So You Want to Be a Novelist

Also by Jon Sealy

The Whiskey Baron
The Edge of America
The Merciful

So You Want to Be a Novelist

to Be a Novelist

a memoir and manifesto

Jon Sealy

Haywire Books
Richmond
Virginia

HAYWIRE BOOKS

Copyright © 2020 by Jon Sealy

ISBN: 9781950182060
Library of Congress Control Number: 2020942280

First Edition

For my parents,
Brian & June

Author's Note

I wrote this book in late 2019 and finished inputting all the copy edits on Friday, March 6, 2020. The following week, everything changed because of the coronavirus. It's impossible to say what the book industry will look like on the other side of this crisis, so I didn't try to revise the book to fit the new industry paradigm or any possible future for Haywire Books.

I suspect all of the pressures I write about on the following pages will be exacerbated—less money to go around, more competition for space on retailers' shelves, fewer opportunities for unknown writers to break out—but I also believe humans are hard-wired for stories. The tagline for Haywire Books is *making sense of a chaotic world*. The world is more chaotic than ever, and we'll need stories in the coming years to explained what just happened to us all.

— Jon Sealy
October 2020

Subjectivity is truth.

— Søren Kierkegaard

CONTENTS

Preface ... 1

The Career ... 5

The Craft ... 83

The Business ... 175

Notes ... 199

PREFACE

In 2019, after years of frustration, I started a small publishing house, Haywire Books, put out my second novel, *The Edge of America*, and published an essay with *The Millions* called "So You Want to Be a Novelist." That essay was couched as an advice piece, and it laid out eighteen years of my process from a college freshman tinkering with stories to an early middle-aged writer still trying to figure things out.

One theme of the essay was the gap between expectations and reality. When you're twenty years old, you have an idea of what it might mean to be a novelist, but the path forward—particularly in the 21st century—is filled with dead ends and disappointments. If you aspire to write capital-A Art, the process requires you to take an honest accounting of yourself and your limitations. This is no easy task in a culture where silence, personal reflection, and deep thinking are in such short supply as to become almost subversive, and where the self has been commodified as a brand. If you read the gurus in publishing—i.e., agents, bloggers, and industry affiliates offering advice on how to be successful—they might tell you that you have to build your platform while you are working on your book, to become an expert or an influencer on a particular subject to prime the publicity pump. That may be good business advice, but it's terrible artistic advice, because it transforms the novel into a purely consumer product, something that can be focus-tested into a bestseller, rather than a nuanced expression of the self.

Meanwhile, the novel has become so culturally marginalized that commercial success has almost no bearing on artistic quality. As a form, the novel is in competition with social media, streaming television, video games, the endless cycle of drama in the news, and more. A good novel is a bit like an introvert trying to stand out in a world of carnival barkers, or a boardroom full of Type A salespeople. That's not to say a high-quality novel can't achieve commercial success, but rather that commercial success is independent from artistic merit—maddening, given that so much of a novelist's professional status, from landing a teaching job to getting the next book contract, are tied to commercial success.

I struggle with whether we are experiencing something new in our era, or if novelists have always felt like the golden days were one generation in the past. Whenever I think it seems as though establishing yourself as a novelist was easier and more lucrative in the 1950s, or even into the 1990s—a brief half-century window in the 20th century when art and commerce aligned—I try to remember Henry James's 1888 novella *The Aspern Papers*. In it, the central character is a scholar who bemoans the fact that no one appreciates high art. The grumpy character sounds just like a group of my writer friends and I when we sit around a campfire complaining about writers who are more successful than we are. Novelists likely have never been satisfied. Whatever the truth of our era, a novelist certainly wears two hats: the artist and the businessperson, and anyone who wants to call herself a novelist is going to have to reckon with those two hats. You have to develop your own definition for what makes a good novel and then write one that satisfies yourself. Then, if you want to be a professional, you have to figure out what you're willing to compromise and how to find an audience for your work.

This book is an expansion of my original essay in *The Millions*. I have in mind my twenty-year-old self, a young would-be writer with a bit of talent and a half-baked notion of what it means to be a novelist. What follows is what I might tell myself, both as a warning and a guide for the road ahead.

I've structured this book into three parts. In part one ("The Career"), I've laid out my own journey from aspirational student to mid-career professional. Every journey may be different, but I think my experience is typical enough to tease out a few lessons. I've also explored some of the issues I've wrestled with—and continue to wrestle with—as a novelist. The conclusion of part one is the story of my starting Haywire Books, which has been an education on the back-end of the industry.

Part two ("The Craft") outlines my understanding of what a novel is and how it works. I've laid out the major elements of fiction, from setting scenes to structuring a plot, and I've explained my own process for writing a novel, which is certainly not the only way to get the job done but may be helpful for a beginner trying to figure out where to start or someone struggling with writers block. You would think the world doesn't need another craft book, but there are some elements of craft that seem lost on even published novelists and their reviewers. The comma-gerund construction, for instance.

Finally, part three ("The Business") is a short overview of the industry in 2020. All I have is my own perspective to go by, but I think it's important for would-be novelists to understand the business they're getting into—what they are offering for sale, where the money goes, and who all is getting paid. The bottom line is that publishing is a tough business for everyone.

I would call the book an *exploration* rather than an *explanation* for how to be a novelist. Everyone's process is different, and every novelist's career is unique. For any guideline I might put down, you could easily point to a counter-example that breaks the rule. To take one silly example, nearly every craft book recommends using "said" to attribute dialogue. "He said," "she said," rather than "exclaimed," "snorted," "scoffed," or "ejaculated." Why does that rule exist? Why do every writing teacher and craft essayist insist on the humdrum "said"? And why do we put up with all those classic novels that employ a variety of dialogue attributions? Although I have an argument for why the "said" rule is—generally—a good one, I'm not here to offer you a prescription. The novel has a remarkable ability to take on more and to reinvent itself as a form—much like the way English over the years has absorbed words from other languages or invented new expressions to match the times. You can always make it new, which is why the form still has life even after the past century of experimentation and development.

Finally, a note about the book's epigraph, Kierkegaard's contention that "Subjectivity is truth." Scores of craft books present "rules" for writing fiction, and some of them do a half-hearted job of explaining why those rules exist, but they seldom disclose the authors' own biases. Everything that follows here is my own subjective view of what a good book is and how I work as a writer. One key theme throughout is the tension between art and commerce, what you produce and consider "good writing," versus what people will pay for and spend time reading. Another way of thinking about this is the tension between writing for yourself versus writing for an audience. Are you producing an expression of yourself, or a consumer product that you can focus-test into bestsellerdom?

I have no answers outside my own life, which is why I've structured this book to lay out my story first. My aesthetic is tied to my own experiences, so if I recommend only using "said" with dialogue attribution, for instance, I have a trunk-load of subjective baggage leading to that recommendation. Same goes if I tell you "gesticulated," "laughed," and "exclaimed" are okay. The only honest way to get at a truth of the craft, I believe, is to give you a peek behind the curtain of my subjective experience, with the idea that you will have to reckon with your own life to develop your own aesthetic. Hemingway once said, "The most essential gift for a good writer is a built-in, shock-proof shit detector." What he didn't add is that it is up to you to find and develop such a detector yourself, so that you may proceed with the business of being a writer. My ultimate conclusion, here, is that you're the one trying to become a novelist, and if you succeed, you're the one who will have to answer to your readers. With that caveat in mind, you're free to do anything you want.

THE CAREER

Beginnings

When my first novel came out in 2014, I had the experience that I suspect many young, would-be novelists dream about, which is I got to give a reading at my alma mater, the College of Charleston. When the book launched, I was feted as the big-deal visiting writer on campus, and I gave my first reading to a room full of creative writing students and my former professors.

After reading a few passages from the book, I gamely answered questions about how to get from there to here, what to do if you want to become a novelist. You know, read a lot, write a lot, don't give up, yadda, yadda, yadda. I was embarrassingly dazzled by the whole experience of being a debut novelist, and was sure my career was on an upward trajectory.

You might be able to guess what happened next: the sophomore slump. After the book tour wound down, I had five years of mostly failures: two books with two agents didn't sell, and meanwhile a new crop of dazzling debut novelists took the literary stage. When I launched my second novel, I was dreading the inevitable question of what to do to get from young scribbler with an idea to a Writer on Book Tour.

Maybe, don't do it.

I was thirty-six years old and had been writing seriously for half my life. In that time, the publishing world became a different game from the one I started playing in college. None of the old rules applied, and I suspected any advice I might offer a student would be irrelevant by the time they found their own way. I started writing this book with the idea that novel writing is such a personal profession that the only timeless lesson might be that you're on your own. The only "advice" I have to offer is a recounting of my own experience in getting from there to here.

The italicized paragraphs that open the following ten chapters are from my original essay, "So You Want to Be a Novelist." I've elaborated on each point to show one process for becoming a novelist. I think my experience is typical enough that it could serve as both a guide and a warning—a guide for getting a toehold in this profession, but also a warning that you, if you are a young would-be novelist, likely are not going to achieve the kind of success you are hoping for. And that's okay.

I like to think about the professional pecking order as a series of concentric rings. In the center, you have maybe a thousand reasonably well paid, reasonably well reviewed novelists. These are the people whose books you will find if you walk into any bookstore in the country, the names you'll see on awards and bestseller lists. The writers you've heard of, in other words.

The second ring contains tens of thousands of professional novelists—writers who are working and likely have one or more traditionally published books, who might teach at a university or may have some small regional acclaim. These are the writers you probably haven't heard of, but it's the most likely ring you will find yourself in if you get into the game of being a novelist. This is where I fall in the pecking order.

The third ring contains a few hundred thousand would-be writers—people who might be writing a novel, or have a manuscript and are seeking an agent, or who are in a writing group with the idea that they may one day write a novel. These are the people populating MFA programs and writing conferences, and flooding agent inboxes with queries.

One key point, in this opening half of the book, is that while it's possible to move from one ring to the next, there's not a whole

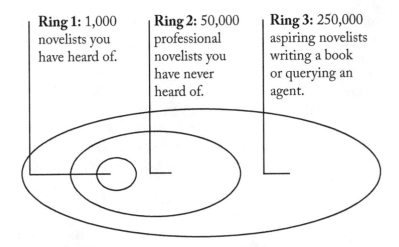

Ring 1: 1,000 novelists you have heard of.

Ring 2: 50,000 professional novelists you have never heard of.

Ring 3: 250,000 aspiring novelists writing a book or querying an agent.

lot of room in the center ring. I suspect everyone who starts out wants to work their way to the center, but the majority of us have to reconcile with living in one of the outer rings. What follows is my story of that reconciliation.

To start at the beginning, one thing I don't like about biographies is that writers spend so much time laying the groundwork for an interesting person's life. A hundred pages about the subject's ancestry, another hundred pages about their childhood, another hundred about college. By the time we get to the interesting stuff—the reason the subject is biography-worthy—time accelerates and it's a bunch of celebrity gossip and health problems until death.

The older I get, however, the more I see how true to life this structure actually is. Those early years from childhood through college burn hot in your memory, and there follows a whirlwind of decades. In this memoir section of the book, I'll try to be as brief as I can, but the early stuff matters. As Flannery O'Connor once quipped, "Anybody who has survived his childhood has enough information about life to last him the rest of his days."

I grew up in Six Mile, South Carolina, a tiny town outside Clemson (home of the Tigers), which is in the upstate not far off I-85 between Atlanta and Charlotte. This part of the state is sometimes called the "dark corner" because for so long it lacked electricity or literacy. When I was growing up, the area was a far cry from the tony publishing world of New York City, but it also wasn't some Rough South backwater that I was lucky to emerge from. I watched plenty of MTV, listened to gangster rap to piss off my parents, and wore a helmet and knee pads while skateboarding. The nearby university provided a semblance of culture, and we had a great local bookstore, the Clemson Newsstand, that provided a window into a world beyond Pickens County.

I didn't write much fiction as a kid, but I did start keeping an occasional journal after reading Beverly Cleary's *Dear Mr. Henshaw*, one of the formative books in my life as a writer. In that novel, the child narrator is writing a journal in the form of letters to a famous author he likes. One year, the school hosts a writing contest, and the narrator submits a story about riding along in his dad's big rig. He doesn't win first prize, but the author judging the contest commends him for writing a realistic story, whereas most of his peers are writing about monsters and aliens. To this day, I'm a committed realist fiction writer, and I think I can safely lay it at the feet of Beverly Cleary.

Although I didn't write much as a child, I've always been a big reader. One of my earliest memories is visiting the local library with my mother. I would sit in the children's section and obsessively reread a book about a mouse and a dragon (I think), while my mother picked out a stack of books from the mysterious adult section. I also remember slinking out of my bedroom after bedtime to sit with my dad on the couch, where I would flip through picture books while he read spy novels late into the evening. I grew up before rise of YA literature, so my reading went from *The Boxcar Children* in elementary school to Stephen King and John Grisham in junior high, with a short transition of reading comic books and the novelizations of R-rated movies my parents wouldn't let me watch. In the summer after seventh grade, we took a family vacation to Arizona. It drove my parents nuts that we flew all the way across the country, and all I wanted to do was sit by the hotel pool and read the novelization of *Die Hard with a Vengeance*.

Key point: You don't have to grow up reading Shakespeare and Homer to become a novelist. Also, there's something subversive, illicit even, about reading fiction.

In high school, I went through the college prep English classes—the middle-of-the-road curriculum for average students. In the 11th and 12th grades, I had a couple of good English teachers for surveys of American and British literature, and seeing the connection between literature and history showed how books could be about more than entertainment. They could help you understand the world and your place in it. I didn't have any great a-ha about committing my life to being a novelist, but I did start thinking there was more to an English curriculum than writing term papers and diagramming sentences. I picked up James Joyce, Hermann Hesse, Hemingway.

Around that time, I also joined the staff of the school literary magazine. Again, this was not about grand literary ambitions, but rather I was attracted to a couple of the girls on staff and wanted an excuse to hang out with them. They were in the AP English track and seemed well-read and cosmopolitan and therefore glamorous.

These days, the majority of people I interact with are ambitious professionals, many of whom have high-achieving high school students at home. These friends, colleagues, and acquaintances all seem bemused—and perhaps don't believe me—when I tell them how little thought I put into college applications. My friends' kids are starting nonprofits in junior high, taking enough AP classes to account for a year of college, touring universities all over the nation, and devising strategies for getting in and earning financial aid. I didn't do any of that.

Most of the people I went to grade school with either didn't go to college, or they went to Clemson or the University of South Carolina. I always assumed I would go to college (though I can't say why), and figured I would end up in something related to engineering (because my dad was an engineer). In my senior year, I applied to Clemson because it was right there. I didn't apply to

South Carolina because of the football rivalry, but I did apply to the College of Charleston because it was a far-off school in a city where I could also get in-state tuition. Finally, I applied to Tulane because they'd sent me some marketing literature. Of the three, CofC offered the best scholarship, so there I went.

It's more complicated than that, of course: I was attracted to a liberal arts school because, having gone through the college prep rather than honors English track, I felt behind in a lot of ways, knowledgeable enough to know there was still a lot I didn't know. But much of my college decision boiled down to convenience and money.

CofC is in downtown Charleston, an old-brick and ivy enclave in the peninsula. In the middle of campus is a big cistern in a courtyard, and to get to the courtyard, you have to go through an archway in a building called Porter's Lodge. Over the archway, inscribed in Greek, is the phrase *Know Thyself*. To apply for the honors college, I had to write an essay about that phrase and what it meant to me. I'm a packrat, so I may still have a copy of that essay on a floppy disc somewhere, but I can't remember what I wrote—probably something obvious about how I believed the purpose of a liberal arts education was to get to know myself—but it got me into the honors college, and I've spent the past two decades thinking about the meaning of that phrase in my life.

1. Know Thyself

Every day you walk by these words inscribed in Greek on an arch on your college campus. You know you love to read, and you believe you are a good writer, so you decide to become a novelist. Understand you are never going to make money in this occupation, and you probably will never find a tenure-track teaching job. Take a hard look at law school. Fork over the money to take the LSAT, just in case. Don't be afraid of a career in real estate. Consider an internship.

For most of us, I'm convinced, finding your way in the world is less about imagination and more about finding models. Growing up, the adults I knew all had nebulous jobs. They worked at the nuclear power plant. They were social workers. They owned various small businesses—auto repair, a bike shop, a Burger King franchise. I certainly didn't know any writers; all the writers I read were either dead (Fitzgerald, O'Connor) or from elsewhere (Stephen King, John Irving). In college, I found my models— older writers doing work I admired, who seemed to provide a blueprint for what one could do with an English degree and how one might live as a fiction writer.

One fall break, I came home from CofC and went to the Clemson Newsstand, where George Singleton and Ron Rash were giving a joint reading. This was 2002, and they were both starting to break out, Singleton with his second book of stories, *The Half Mammals of Dixie*, and Rash with his first novel, *One Foot in Eden*. I was familiar with both of them; Singleton had taught one of my high school friends at the regional governor's school; Rash's wife had been my high school American literature teacher, and I'd read a few of his poems. But it wasn't until I saw them reading together, and heard them discuss books and writing in the Q&A portion of the evening, that I understood what was possible in the world of fiction writing.

One Foot in Eden is set a few miles from where I grew up, and is about a murder in the 1950s. The local power company had dammed up the Jocassee River and was flooding the valley, and the body was buried in the rising water. Rash read from a section narrated by a woman who had been impregnated by the victim, talking to her husband, who might have been the killer, about the baby. The rhythms of the prose, the description of the landscape and the flora, the complex situation these characters had found themselves in: I was hooked.

Then, Singleton read a story called "This Itches, Y'all," about a guy looking back on his years in the South Carolina educational system, when as a child he'd starred in a public service video about head lice. His line in the video was, "This itches, y'all," and into adulthood his old classmates would repeat that line back to him and scratch their heads. He'd long thought they were making fun of him, and it took him into adulthood to come to terms with where he was living and how he fit in. The story was hilarious, but also had a ton of heart. A man trying to reckon with mixed feelings about where he came from: this could have been my story.

For years afterward, most of my fiction read like knockoff Singleton and Rash. Poetic descriptions of the Carolina upstate combined with zany characters in weird situations.

At the time, Rash was teaching at the local technical college, and Singleton was at the governor's school. Teaching seemed to be a logical way of making a living while being able to write artful fiction on the side. An English teacher I knew clued me in that short stories were published in magazines called literary journals, so perhaps on that same fall break home, I picked up a stack of journals from the Newsstand—*The Georgia Review, The Southern Review, The Virginia Quarterly Review*. I found an interview with Singleton online where he said his first story was published in

The Greensboro Review, so I promptly sent a short story their way, which they rejected nearly as promptly.

So began a slow and grinding career.

Another important model from those years was my college fiction professor, Bret Lott. He ran a traditional writing workshop, where everyone in class turned in two stories a semester, and when you were up, we spent half the class period discussing the piece. What's working, what's not working, what strategies might the writer use for revision, and so on. I remember the stories I wrote for his class, and I remember he straightened out a few bad habits of mine, mostly around point of view.

More than anything, however, I remember his fundamental philosophy that fiction is about discovery. His class motto was *I know nothing*, which for him meant two things. First, quite literally, while writing the story, you were supposed to follow a character without knowing where the story might take you. You weren't supposed to make assumptions about what the story was about, or what was motivating the character, or even your own point of view of the situation. Lott would cite Flannery O'Connor, who in her book *Mystery and Manners* writes that "there is a certain grain of stupidity that the writer of fiction can hardly do without, and this is the quality of having to stare, of not getting the point at once." She later discusses her story "Good Country People," which is about a bible salesman who tries to seduce a disabled woman with a Ph.D. At the end of the story, he makes off with her wooden leg, an event O'Connor says she didn't see coming: "As the story progressed, I brought in the Bible salesman, but I had no idea what I was going to do with him. I didn't know he was going to steal that wooden leg until ten or twelve lines before he did it, but when I found out that this was what was going to happen, I realized that it was inevitable."

The second thing Lott meant with his *I know nothing* motto was more elemental. He connected the act of writing to Socratic wisdom. Back in ancient Greece, an oracle told Socrates he was the wisest man, which he didn't believe. Socrates went around asking questions of the town's allegedly wisest men—the judges and lawyers and politicians and such—but by peppering them with questions, Socrates revealed them to be fools full of hot air. He really was the wisest man because he had an appropriate sense of self-doubt, an open mind, and curiosity. These values are imperative for a fiction writer because as soon as you stop saying *I know*, and consider the possibility that you don't know, that you could be wrong, you suddenly see the world with greater clarity.

These values—doubt, openness, curiosity—are antithetical to the thrust of American culture in 2020. In the business world where I operate in my day job, leaders obscure the facts of their operations with a veil of buzzwords—*innovation, data-driven analytics, consumer centricity*—that mean nothing in themselves. Meanwhile in politics, you have hypocrites on the right shrieking about fake news, while on the left you have ideological hard-liners issuing purity tests. Both sides are equally sure of themselves, and are equally foolish, whereas the good fiction writer operates in the gray area, in the messy middle.

I would be remiss to talk about my college fiction workshop without mentioning my wife, Emily, whom I met and got to know in Lott's fiction workshop our junior year. This is a book about becoming a novelist, but becoming a novelist, for me, means making art out of the stuff of life—taking what you see and feel and experience, putting it through the sifter of your brain, and transmogrifying it into a fictional narrative. You would be hard-pressed to find Emily on the page in any of my novels, but nothing I've written would have been the same without her in my life. The sense of openness, curiosity, and healthy self-doubt are conducive to finding a good mate, if that's something you want out of life, and I believe a good mate can help you maintain those values when it would be easier to shut down, close your mind, and just go make money.

Key point: How you live matters as much as what you do. As James Baldwin once wrote, "People pay for what they do, and still more for what they have allowed themselves to become, and they pay for it very simply: by the lives they lead."

I would also be remiss not to mention the CofC English department at large. I'm not sure what the department's curriculum looks like today, but at the time it was quite old-fashioned as far as English departments went. The degree required taking classes from different eras, and most of the old guard of professors took a "close reading approach" to literature. For instance, Nan Morrison taught Shakespeare the way Shakespeare had been taught for ages, by studying it scene by scene and word by word. She might have thrown in some historical context, but the focus was on the text itself—the language, the character development, the drama. My adviser, Larry Carlson, discussed the unpredictability of what gets canonized (citing as an example the forgotten writer Joseph Hergesheimer, to whom Sinclair Lewis dedicated *Main Street*), but he also walked his classes through the language of *Moby-Dick* and the psychology of *A Portrait of a Lady*.

I understand the push in academia to deconstruct the old white guy canon, but I do feel grateful to have gone through an English curriculum that emphasized literary texts over culture and politics. I don't meant to disparage the research or philosophy of someone who wants to structure a course around, say, "Borders in American Fiction" or "Deconstructing Gender Norms in Shakespeare," but if the course becomes about the topic (historical, philosophical, political, socio-cultural) rather than the texts, I don't believe it's the best training for a writer. A writer in training would do well to read dusty old New Critical texts such as Ian Watts's *The Rise of the Novel*. Or, for a more modern, progressive version, Jane Smiley's *13 Ways of Looking at the Novel* is an ideal introduction to the novel—its form, its history, and how it works from the inside.

The fiction writer traffics in words and images, not ideas, at least in the first draft. Flannery O'Connor again, this time explicating a passage from *Madame Bovary* in which Flaubert describes a man as wearing a particular type of slipper: "It's always necessary to remember that the fiction writer is much less *immediately* concerned with grand ideas and bristling emotions than he is with putting list slippers on clerks." The job of the fiction writer is to describe first, to ask the question without necessarily answering it. As Chekhov said in a letter to a fellow writer, "You are right in demanding that an artist should take an intelligent attitude to his work, but you confuse two things: solving a problem and stating a problem correctly. It is only the second that is obligatory for the artist."

You can't separate art from culture, literature from history, but just as a good painter needs training in the technique of mixing colors, or a musician needs to learn the scales, a writer needs training in the craft of bringing scenes to life with words.

Like Singleton and Rash, Lott was a teacher, and he seemed to me to be living a very nice life. An office filled with books on a beautiful university campus, a class he could walk outside and teach while smoking a cigar, a new novel published every three years. His life was more complicated than it seemed, of course, which he recounts in his book of essays *Before We Get Started*. In it, he lays out his philosophy of fiction and discusses his own path through rejection. It's an excellent book for any would-be writer.

To plan my own career, I looked at the lives of the prominent fiction writers I was reading, and the majority of them had a Master of Fine Arts, or MFA, in creative writing. The career path seemed to be:

(a) Get an MFA.
(b) Start publishing short stories in the literary magazines.
(c) Teach a heavy load of composition for a few years while you finished a novel.
(d) Publish the novel and get a tenure-track teaching job.
(e) Live a great life.

I had no idea just how many young writers such as myself were coming to that same conclusion, and would soon flood the market with their degrees and ambitions. All I knew was that my next step in that sequence would be the MFA. My senior year, Lott took a job editing *The Southern Review*, so I worked with CofC's poetry professor at the time, Carol Ann Davis, on an independent study to pull a manuscript together for graduate school applications. Davis shared many of Lott's general ideas around fiction, though as a poet she emphasized writing as a way of exploring your own brain, where the audience is almost incidental to the work itself (though I don't remember her putting it in quite those terms). As you'll gather throughout this book, audience is a recurring theme for the fiction writer: who are you writing for? Are you writing for anyone? How will you balance your personal art with the demands of the market?

I spent about as much energy researching graduate schools as I did colleges, which is to say I did almost nothing. I think I applied to eight schools, mostly places where CofC graduates had been accepted and that I knew had teaching fellowships. Listen: I'm sure I had heard of the Iowa Writers Workshop, which is the oldest and most esteemed writing program in the country, but I don't think it even occurred to me to apply there. That's how little research I did. I seem to remember Davis at one point saying you only want to go to a school that will pay you to go there, which might be the best practical advice anyone ever gave me in this career.

Purdue University accepted me early, and after learning they had a teaching fellowship that would cover all my tuition and give me a stipend—enough to live on, if you could live with couple of roommates in a cheap house next to a meth dealer. I signed up, withdrew the rest of my applications, and spent the rest of my senior year reading Gabriel Garcia Marquez, drinking a little too heavily, and waiting for the next thing. Over the summer, I moved home to Six Mile for a few weeks where, unemployed, I wrote a novel in eight weeks.

2. Go to Graduate School

Or don't. It doesn't really matter where you go. All that matters is what you do there—namely, read a lot and write a lot. Maybe take advantage of staying on your parents' health insurance plan and spend your early twenties doing some mind-numbing job. Wash dishes, perhaps. Or serve coffee. Just don't take on debt. Commit to reading 100 pages and writing 1,000 words a day, at least five days a week. Write a novel. Revise it. Revise it. Revise it. If you can swing it, consider paying a good editor a goodly sum to give you a professional critique. That'll save you some time.

This isn't original to me, but success in any endeavor tends to boil down to a combination of aptitude, hard work, and luck. I don't know how productive it is to theorize around *aptitude*—or, if you prefer, *talent*—but I do think things come easier to some writers. It's not fair, but there's nothing you can do about it except try to do the best with the abilities you do have. Based on my own experience and the writers I know, *hard work* makes up for many shortcomings—great news, because work is the only thing you're in control of. Finally, *luck* comes in two forms: stumbling on the right idea at the right time (which you can prepare for) and then having the right combination of things happen on the commercial side (which you will likely have to reckon with, and which almost certainly won't go your way even if you find great commercial success).

So, *hard work* then is the subject at hand, the one element of your career you are truly in charge of. Unfortunately, it's also the piece that aspiring writers have the most trouble with. Most would-be writers I've met—in university classes, at conferences, or simply in passing—don't want to put in the time to read deeply, don't want to sit in the chair, and don't want to crank out the pages. I certainly understand, but the dismal truth is that work as a writer is a bit like investing. You see compound returns over time, and you can never get your time back. There is something of a Writing Industrial Complex around the world of MFAs, writing conferences, blogging culture, and even this very book you are reading—and none of it is a shortcut around the work itself.

What does work look like? The best example I know is the story of the writer Larry Brown—a story recounted by Barry Hannah in the preface to Brown's posthumous final novel, *A Miracle of Catfish*, and by Jonathan Miles in the introduction to Brown's collected stories, *Tiny Love*.

After nearly flunking high school English, Brown joined the Marines and then knocked around a few jobs before becoming a firefighter in Oxford, Mississippi. When he was 29 years old (around 1980), he decided he wanted to become a writer to work with his mind rather than his hands. He borrowed his wife's typewriter and went to work, writing when things were slow on his shift as a firefighter, writing at home, writing all night, writing all the time. By his own admission, Brown had no talent to speak of, and his first (unpublished) novel was 400 single-spaced pages about a man-eating bear in Yellowstone. He went on to write another four unpublished novels plus more than a hundred short stories. He befriended the writer Barry Hannah, who wrote of his friend, "In the early eighties he showed me stories that were so bad, I'd duck out the back of the bar when I saw him coming down the walk with the inevitable manila envelope. I couldn't stand to hurt his feelings."

In his introduction to *Tiny Love*, Miles sheds additional light on what Brown was doing in his self-directed apprenticeship: "Larry wrote ghost stories, Westerns, Civil War stories, African hunting tales, and detective stories. He wrote tongue-in-cheek outdoors instruction (under the pen name Uncle Whitney) and essays about gun safety, coon hunting, and lingerie." Brown was almost entirely self-taught, but as Hannah and Miles both note, his apprenticeship involved deep reading and lots and lots of writing. What strikes me most, today, about Brown's story is the range of stories he wrote. His published oeuvre reads of a piece, in the realistic southern "grit lit" mode. Working class people struggling to do their best while making bad choices in a world that doesn't always forgive them. Until I read Miles's essay, it never occurred to me that Brown had written ghost stories. Imagine!

Key point: Not everything you write needs to be in your genre, and not everything you write needs to be published. In fact, it may be helpful to plan on writing one or more practice novels.

Looking back on my own apprenticeship, I would say I did the work. I wrote a lot in my twenties, but I didn't write as much as Larry Brown. Now that I understand how time constricts on you as you get older, and how other obligations restrict the energy you can dedicate to the work, and how writing operates like an investment, offering compound returns as you age, I still can't help but wish I'd done more.

Most writers I went through school with were fiddlers. A sample graduate writing workshop might require students to turn in three stories a semester, and my sense is most writers look at those deadlines as their quota for the semester. Three good stories a semester gives you twelve stories over two years, which is pretty close to book length but a far cry from Brown's five apprentice novels and 100+ short stories. I think producing three stories a semester leads to a mentality that the job is to write *only* three stories a semester, and to make them perfect by fiddling with them—shade the character here, transpose the sentence structure there, rewrite the ending a dozen times. I admire the attention to detail of a fiddler, but that mentality can be paralyzing for a novelist, at least in the early years.

The (primarily) short story writer George Singleton has written an excellent book of writing aphorisms, *Pep Talks, Warnings, and Screeds*. In it, he discusses the difference between what he calls "shotgun writers" and "sharpshooter writers." The shotgun writer, Singleton explains, will blast out dozens of stories a year, and once they get established they will likely publish half a dozen a year. Meanwhile, the sharpshooter writer will fiddle and fiddle and fiddle and produce only a couple of stories a year—but one of them may end up in *The New Yorker*. I think novelists-in-training would likely be well served to aspire toward the shotgun method.

At the end of his book of aphorisms, Singleton has a longer essay about how to be a shotgun short story writer. He advises you move out to the country, start walking around to collect beer cans off the side of the road, and write one 5,000-word short story a week, every week, for twenty years or so. Then you will have made it. Maintaining that kind of pace is hard work. I might suggest that while you *may* see success without that kind of grueling schedule, you almost certainly *will* see some kind of success if you can follow Singleton's (and Brown's) blueprints.

When I went to graduate school, I had Brown's biography in mind—the idea that I may need to write a few practice novels before I got published. I also had something in mind I heard Singleton say at a bookstore reading, perhaps that original reading in 2002 where he read "This Itches, Y'all." Someone in the audience asked him about getting published, and Singleton said one of his early mentors told him he would have to write 1,000 pages before he got something published. Of course, he thought he would beat that, no problem, but he said that sure enough it took him two bad novels and a handful of stories before *The Greensboro Review* picked up his first story.

At a departmental reception at CofC, I once cornered Bret Lott to ask him for any personal advice for me, and he said his main recommendation would be to read everything I could get my hands on.

So, read a lot (per Bret Lott) and write a lot (per George Singleton).

This is also the advice in Stephen King's memoir *On Writing*, in which he advises you to write 2,500 words a day. I read and reread King's book in college and kept it close while I wrote the first draft of my own first novel. In the summer after college, I'd been kicking around the idea of writing a novel, and I felt like if I were going to go to graduate school and commit myself to some kind of literary life, I owed it to myself to see if I had it in me to actually do it. I set myself a goal of writing 10,000 words a week for the summer, and every day I would get up and go to the Clemson University library, descend a few levels into the basement where they kept the American literature. There I would read a few pages of the old masters in the PS section of the Library of Congress Classification System, and then I would do my best to crank out 2,500 words. Some weeks, I had my 10,000 words by Thursday and enjoyed a weekend out with friends. Other weeks I was grinding away on Sunday night to get through the last thousand words.

The book was about a teenage girl who gets involved with a bad-news boy. It was … pretty bad. I must have known it, too, because I immediately put it in a drawer and started writing a new novel about a man on the run after burying a body. I got about fifty pages into that novel, which was set in a Depression-era textile mill town, before I realized I would need to do some research before doing much more with it. Instead, I stopped working on novels for two years and worked on short stories for my MFA workshops. I wrote more than the requisite three stories per semester, yet I am not a natural short story writer. It may seem counterintuitive, but I don't have the patience to write short. I get bored. There's a common saying that writing short stories has more in common with writing poetry than it does with writing novels, and that makes sense to me. With a novel, you have one story to dig into every day for months on end. With a story or poem, you have to invent a new image, a new character, a new plot every week. I don't know how story writers and poets do it.

To get an MFA or not to get an MFA? That debate flares up on Twitter every few years, with the next crop of MFA graduates weighing in. I don't regret my experience. I met a few of my best friends there, and I had plenty of time to write and read and think deeply about books. With Singleton and Lott's advice in mind, I set myself a goal of writing a thousand words and reading a hundred pages a day, five days a week, a pace I would keep up for most of my twenties.

But if I knew then what I know now, I might have done something different. Gotten a job washing dishes, perhaps, or kept working for a coffee shop in Charleston where I worked during school. I might have plowed through the 1930s murder novel, and then written yet another novel. Maybe saved or borrowed $2,000 for a very good professional critique from a freelance editor. Maybe attended the Sewanee Writers Conference to gain a few connections in the literary world and talk with some agents. And kept going. As the story of Larry Brown suggests, you certainly don't need an MFA to learn the craft of writing.

The MFA does give you time to write, and it also makes you feel part of the game. In addition to the workshops themselves, I got to meet and mingle with visiting writers, worked on the staff of the *Sycamore Review*, and generally had something to say about my life as a writer when I went home for holidays. As I would find out soon enough, it's difficult to maintain the pose of Being a Writer when you are just working in the world like your average Joe, not publishing or doing the kinds of things that make you feel like a real writer. Since I was on staff with the literary journal, I attended the AWP conference a few times, where I started to build a small network of peers, and I became familiar with the world of literary magazines, which was so much larger than what I found at the old Clemson Newsstand. It's an entire sub-culture, and one that can help sustain you when you're "writing out in the cold," as Ted Solotaroff put it.

The world has changed so much even in the short period since I went through my MFA program that I no longer feel comfortable offering a full evaluation of the experience, but I do feel confident recommending no one go into debt to get an MFA. Once debt enters the picture, the experience becomes a financial investment, and you almost certainly will not see any material returns on it as an investment. Employers in corporate America need the skillset of someone with an MFA—analytical skills, creative writing, empathy, the ability to work on deadline—but it doesn't seem like there's much, if any, focus in the MFA universe around professionalization outside academia. How to translate your skills into something a corporation might want. How to build a stable of clients as a freelance writer. The practical business of feeding yourself. These are things you'll have to figure out on your own.

One thing a young writer won't find is a tenure-track teaching job. When I was 22, I thought the MFA was the first step toward an academic life, but teaching is its own separate profession. You need aptitude, hard work, and luck to make it in that life, and it's a different kind of aptitude, a different kind of work. At Purdue I taught freshman composition and a few semesters of creative writing, but I didn't have much aptitude as a teacher, and I wasn't willing to put in the work it takes to do well in that profession. I wish there were more discourse about teaching as a profession, rather than something writers do while pursuing their creative efforts. Such a discourse from within the academy might be a good counter-weight to the broader American trend of reducing teachers to commodities, service workers whose job is to babysit the young and administer standardized tests, which is how some politicians seem to view the profession.

More on point, I think most professionals in the MFA universe now understand the Ponzi-like nature of the system, how there are too many programs cranking out too many graduates for even a small fraction of them to land a cushy teaching job. Perhaps the norms within MFA programs are changing, but I would strongly counsel young novelists against taking on any debt to finance the degree. Take that money and use it to hire a freelance book editor and attend a couple of conferences where you can meet agents. The program won't offer you anything you can't find on your own, provided you put in the work.

3. Watch Your Dreams Disintegrate

Send the book out to 50 agents. Don't get heartbroken when they tell you they can't sell it because it's too "quiet." No one asked you to write a novel, and no one wants to read it, and anyway this first one's not any good. Don't take up smoking. Try not to drink too much. Remember Beckett's quote: "Try again. Fail again. Fail better." Read and reread Ted Solotaroff's essay "Writing in the Cold." Write another novel.

Ted Solotaroff was an American writer, critic, and literary magazine editor. He wrote an essay called "Writing in the Cold," in which he reflected on the unpredictable nature of a literary career. He opens the essay:

> During the decade of editing *New American Review*, I was often struck by how many gifted young writers there were in America. They would arrive every month, three or four of them, accomplished or close to it, full of wit and panache or a steady power or a fine, quiet complexity. We tried to devote twenty-five per cent of each issue to these new voices and seldom failed to meet the quota. Where were they all coming from?

He then asks, "What happened to all of that bright promise?" He noted that about half of the young writers he published disappeared over the next ten years, about a quarter had reasonably successful literary careers, and the final quarter had marginal careers.

Now that I'm more than ten years out of my MFA program, I've thought a lot about Solotaroff's essay, and about the writers I've known over the years, and where we've all ended up. When I was in college, I started my English curriculum feeling behind—the rube from Six Mile who hadn't taken AP English in high school, couldn't write a line of iambic pentameter, and had little to say about literature beyond what the professors were telling me. By the time I graduated, I felt like I was somewhere in the upper third of the pack. Not the smartest literature student, but I had a talent for writing and had gained some confidence.

Then, in graduate school, I felt like I was toward the bottom of the pack again. I had a strong literary background, but most of my peers had taken a few years off between college and the MFA, so they were older and had some life experience, and they were all very strong writers. Again, by the time I graduated, I felt like I was in the upper half of the pack. I'd put in the work to write an entire novel, I'd done some extracurricular work with *Sycamore Review*, I'd improved as a writer. In my last semester of workshop, I turned in the first chapter of the teenage girl novel, and the class generally agreed the story might work better if it incorporated some of her father's perspective. Looking back, my original story might have made a fine YA novel, but the YA genre hadn't taken off in 2007, so I set about radically revising the book over the third year of my MFA. I graduated with a complete and revised novel ready (I thought) for the literary agents.

Then came the period that Solotaroff was writing about, the ten years "out in the cold," away from peers who support you and an institution offering a sheen of professional cover. The program director, Porter Shreve, suggested, somewhat off hand, that the most important time in your MFA program was actually the summer after, because that's the summer that determines whether you keep writing or decide you want to go to law school. I took that to heart and started sending my MFA thesis out to literary agents, applied to some conferences, and finally wrote a first draft of the 1930s mill novel that I'd been researching.

*

It might seem, from the paragraph above, that I was moving into the next phase of the chute, still on the slow train to success. One of my favorite quotes comes from the writer William Gibson, who said, "The future is already here—it's just not very evenly distributed." He was referring to technology, but I think it applies to everything in life. In 2008, much of the future in publishing was already here: Amazon was taking over the book market, Netflix was getting into the streaming television business, Facebook had expanded beyond colleges and universities, self-publishing was on the rise, and the financial collapse was happening. The staid old book industry profession I thought I was getting into was in the midst of being up-ended, but few people truly understood it.

In my personal life, the future was already written, to some degree, though I had no way of recognizing it. Emily—my girlfriend from the College of Charleston—was in a graduate theater program in Richmond, Virginia, and she was interested in law school. I was interested in marrying her, so I moved from Indiana to Virginia, which severely limited my options in academia. What's more, because I had not put in the extra work as a teacher while in my MFA program, I had a couple of letters of recommendation but lacked any sense of how academic hiring worked. Somehow, I lucked into one adjunct teaching gig in Richmond, but it wouldn't pay enough bills to cover rent. I started papering the town with job applications, and quickly discovered I had no idea what I was qualified to do or where I might look for work. I focused on retail and food service because that's the kind of work I knew, and because the shifts would be flexible enough to accommodate teaching a three-day-a-week comp class. When I hadn't gotten any callbacks after a few weeks, I started to suspect that having a master's degree on my resume was a liability. I left the MFA off an application to Circuit City and promptly got hired as a salesman.

If you vaguely remember Circuit City, you might remember it was at one time a solid American company. Headquartered in Richmond, it made it into Jim Collins's business classic *Good to Great* as a case study of success. You might remember the jingle from the nineties, *Welcome to Circuit City, where service is state of the art*. And you might remember the salespeople wearing polo shirts and looking somewhat respectable. If you really remember Circuit City, you might know they got into financial trouble in the mid-2000s, and tried to solve the issue by laying off all their experienced, commissioned salespeople and hiring inexperienced bozos like me for $8 an hour.

I can't impress upon you how ill equipped I was to sell consumer electronics. I had a flip phone that was free with my Verizon plan, a Macbook computer, a tape deck in my truck, and a TV/VCR combo I'd been lugging around since high school. I couldn't tell you what an LCD TV was or why you might want one instead of a plasma screen. I couldn't tell you what kind of processor you needed in a PC, or even how to operate Microsoft Vista. And I'd never heard of an HDMI cable. There wasn't anything in that store I knew how to sell, but desperation will give you the ability to fake enthusiasm in a job interview, and the Circuit City employee's job in 2008 primarily entailed trying to stay out of sight of the manager, lest he scream into the headpiece in your ear, "I have a guest by the laptops who needs help." The best place to hide was by the car stereos, so after a few weeks of talking to the guys who installed that stuff, I was able to pick up enough lingo to help anyone who needed a CD player. Plus, the company gave out free installations, which meant I got to ring up the Firedog service bundle, which made my sales numbers look great without actually having to do anything.

I say all this because this is the reality for the life of an adjunct teacher. This is the life you might be signing up for if you are a college student thinking about an MFA and a life in academia. I turned twenty-six that fall, I had a master's degree, and three days a week I would wake up, make a pot of coffee, drive to an upscale university campus, teach the principles of rhetoric to well-educated and well-heeled students from Connecticut, and then I would slip on a goofy red t-shirt, tuck it into a pair of jeans, drive over to the store, and clock in to work alongside bored teenagers who wanted to talk about video games. I had one student email me about getting a discount on an Xbox, but thank God none of them ever came into the store. My manager would have sent me over to sell them something and then given me a hassle if I didn't try to upsell them on overpriced cables.

Things didn't get much better into the fall, when the financial system blew up and sent us spiraling into the Great Recession. In late September, my bank, Wachovia, failed. A few weeks later, the university where I was teaching announced the restructuring of its freshman experience. They would be doing away with introductory composition, which meant I was out of a teaching job. Then, a few weeks later, Circuit City filed for bankruptcy. I was out one bank and two jobs, and didn't understand anything that was going on in the broader economy. I vaguely understood the housing crisis, but couldn't connect it to mortgage-backed securities (whatever they were) and the credit crunch. All I knew was that people were talking about this being the worst crisis since the Great Depression, a period I understood to some degree thanks to all my research into the Carolina textile mills.

I started reading up on economics and continued writing a draft of what would become my first published novel, *The Whiskey Baron*. I also started looking for new jobs. Not having any professional models outside academia, I looked to the only other place I knew writers worked: the local newspaper. I landed a job with the *Richmond Times-Dispatch*, where I did everything from proofreading to interviewing car dealers to writing a column in the Sunday wedding section. The pay wasn't great, but it was twice what I was making as an adjunct teacher slash car stereo salesman, so I thought I'd peaked as a human being. At the beginning of 2009, I was on my way to getting married, I had a five-figure job, and I had health insurance.

Then the recession and the loss of classified advertising caught up to the newspaper. A few weeks into my new job, they laid off ten percent of the company and gave the rest of us a few weeks of unpaid furlough.

While I was trying to find purchase in a collapsing world, I was also trying to get my literary career off the ground. I sent my thesis novel, *Issaqueena*, off to about fifty agents that summer and fall of 2008. A few asked to read the manuscript, but the only feedback they gave me was that it was too "quiet" for them to sell.

Jon Sealy

It took a long time for me to see that novel for what it was, which was a well written but ultimately plotless book about a man I didn't understand and his daughter, who I did understand but whose age bracket I was losing touch with every year.

In the realm of luck, I think if I had come of age as a writer in the seventies or eighties, I might have found a publisher for that novel. It was in the vein of books from that era—Jayne Anne Phillips's *Machine Dreams* and Bobbie Ann Mason's *In Country* and Charles Baxter's *Shadow Play*. It wasn't as good as those novels, but it had enough going for it that an editor of that era probably could have helped shape it into a respectable debut book. Alas, I came of age as a novelist in the 21st century, so I decided that for my next book, I would write a "loud" novel. I'd always loved crime fiction, so I took my story of this mill family and a man on the run, and I dropped a brutal murder on page 1, two boys shot in front of a bootlegger's speakeasy. With the Great Recession in full swing and my mind on economics, I also had an idea for a South Florida crime novel in the vein of Graham Greene.

Although I wasn't doing my best work—still an apprentice, in many ways—I think I'll always look back at 2009 as the best writing year of my life. Those were what they call salad days. The newspaper only gave me two weeks of vacation, so the extra three weeks of furlough were welcome. My hours were 10 a.m. to 6 p.m., so I was able to get up every day and write for a couple of hours before going to the office. In fall 2009, the university still hadn't completed its restructuring, so they hired me to teach another class, which I did at eight in the morning before my shift at the paper. I spent most of my furlough days languishing in the university library, still getting rejected by agents for *Issaqueena* but working on two novels—*The Whiskey Baron* and the South Florida novel that would become *The Edge of America*. I reread all of Cormac McCarthy, read all the big Latin American novels I'd put off studying, saw my first short story in print, and had the occasional by-line in the newspaper.

It all felt like I was *becoming*, to use Michelle Obama's word.

Or, in Beckett's phrasing, *Try again. Fail again. Fail better.*

32

4. Double Down

Revise the new novel. Make it scream! Send it out to 100 agents. Try not to get discouraged when no one wants this one either. Bite your tongue when a famous agent tells you it's too "depressing." Have faith: a few years later, someone on Goodreads will say the same thing in a review. It's okay to get married, get a real job, and buy a house in the suburbs. Remember Flaubert's dictum: "Be regular and orderly in your life like a bourgeois, so that you may be violent and original in your work." Maybe take another look at law school, or write three more novels.

There's a little bit of a snowball effect that happens in the writing business. Success breeds success (and, possibly, failure may breed failure). Every professional probably needs that first lucky break—that first mentor, that first internship, that first job—and then sees one thing lead to the next as a career takes shape.

My first published short story was one of my MFA workshop stories called "Renovation," a piece roughly about a landscaping job I'd had during a couple of summers in college. A pair of Purdue graduates from yester-year had started a new online literary journal called *Freight Stories*, and I sent it to them with a mention that I'd recently graduated from Purdue. I don't know if it was purely the story itself, or the Purdue connection, or the fact that I'd workshopped the story with Patricia Henley (and therefore it had a sheen of her aesthetic baked into it, the very aesthetic the editors were looking for), but they accepted it and published it in late 2008.

Around that time, I'd started a blog and put up a link to the story. An editor from *The Sun* magazine read the story, found my blog, and sent me a note saying she enjoyed it. I took a look at my material on hand, carved out an excerpt from *The Whiskey Baron*, and sent it that editor for consideration, and *The Sun* accepted it for publication in 2011. I've had that publication in my bio ever since, and I suspect having an excerpt of the novel in *The Sun* was one point in my favor when I got in touch with the editor at Hub City Press in 2012. Another big point in my favor was I'd asked my old fiction professor at CofC, Bret Lott, to look at the novel, and he gave it a generous "pre-blurb," a.k.a., endorsement.

It feels a little slimy discussing the way these things happen, how one accolade or personal connection can lead to another opportunity, but I'd be lying if I said it didn't work like that. What I will say, though, is that you don't need a long pedigree to get into the game of publishing—that middle concentric circle of 50,000 or so professional novelists. Nor does a young writer need to spend too much energy cynically trying to make connections. Building a network and finding opportunities can happen—and I would argue, should happen—organically over a number of years. The bread crumbs that eventually led to my first published novel ranged from taking a workshop with Lott in 2003, writing a story for Henley's workshop in 2005, submitting that story to *Freight Stories* in 2008, submitting another story to *The Sun* in 2010, and stumbling onto Hub City in 2012 with the right book and the right qualifications at the right time.

It might have been faster—and I might have seen more success by this point in my life—had I been the son of a famous novelist or book publisher, or if I'd gone to Brown and married a gal who would become a literary agent, or if I'd dropped eighty grand on an MFA from Columbia. Then again, had that been my story, I might right now be losing my hair in Brooklyn, working on a novel about other people in Brooklyn grumbling about rent and their relationships, and waking up at 2 a.m. from the crushing weight of student loan payments I will never be able to pay back.

Key point: You take what you have to work with, and you keep showing up. Learn to write well. Write all the time. Write some more. Be kind to people. Have patience.

When I finished writing *The Whiskey Baron*, I really did double down. I'd sent *Issaqueena* to fifty agents, so I made a list of a hundred agents and sent letters out in batches of ten. I read all the blogs about how to pitch agents, I split-test my query letter, I did all the things. And I had a great response. Out of the fifty agents I queried for *Issaqueena*, I think only three or so asked to read it. Out of the hundred agents for *The Whiskey Baron*, around twenty-five ask to read it. Some of them were Very Famous Agents. Six-figure deal-making agents.

No one told me it was "quiet," but no one wanted to represent it, either, and no one gave me enough substantial feedback for me to do anything with the novel. One guy told me it was "too depressing" to break out as a first novel, and maybe he had a point. After the double murder that opens the book, an old sheriff comes out to investigate, and the investigation pits him against a villainous whiskey baron whose empire is collapsing around him. Caught in the middle is a family of textile workers struggling to get by. The book is told from multiple points of view, making it less of a "whodunnit" and more of a "why-dunnit" or a "what happens now" story. A future agent would tell me my work is "caught between two chairs," not fully in a genre lane (and therefore not a good mystery) but also not quite a literary novel.

I'm proud of *The Whiskey Baron*, but I see its limitations, both as a work of art and as a commercial product. What can you do about that? I keep coming back to this idea that you can't control your aptitude. Sometimes your best isn't enough to land a book deal with Knopf, but all you can do is keep showing up. Keep doing the work. While I was doubling down with the submissions, I drafted and revised *The Edge of America*, I wrote a mess of a novel that was a kinda-sorta sequel to *The Whiskey Baron*, and I wrote a straight-up mystery set in rural Indiana.

Pages kept piling up.

One theory I have about publishing is that it takes a few novels for you to find your voice, and for you to find your audience. When I was starting out, I read everybody's first novel to see where they started and what moves they made. These days, I seldom enjoy first novels because I know all the moves and wrong turns that can happen in your first book, or even your first few books. On the other hand, there's something uniquely satisfying about reading a novelist at the top of her game, three, five, seven books in. The prose becomes more supple, more natural, and the stories become somehow both familiar and strange.

A few examples: One of my favorite novels in recent years is Steve Yarbrough's *The Unmade World*, which is about a man whose wife and daughter are killed in a hit and run in Poland. The novel follows the widower and the driver in parallel narratives over the next decade. Yarbrough is a Mississippi native, and his first several novels were in the "grit lit" mode of southern fiction. Tough guys, working class characters, the Big Issues of the South. Somewhere along the way—perhaps it was the author moving to Boston late in his career—Yarbrough became more expansive. His novels read less like Larry Brown and more like Richard Yates. *The Unmade World* moves fluidly through time and across geography (Poland to California to New England) in a way that is difficult to pull off. Moreover, because the story has twin narratives, you assume from the beginning there's only a couple of ways it can end. Either these characters, the driver and the victim, will meet again, or they won't. What Yarbrough does at the end of the novel is more nuanced, and surprising—an ending I don't think an early-career novelist would have been able to manage.

Another example: Jami Attenberg's most recent novel, *All This Could Be Yours*, is about a dying patriarch, and the family converges on New Orleans in his last days. The grown daughter, Alex, is trying to understand her father and her parents' marriage, and is angling for information from her reticent mother. Her brother is refusing to come home from L.A., so the sister-in-law, Twyla, is representing them—and has her own complex story. The plot is straightforward enough, but Attenberg employs a fascinating voice, a rolling style with commas and asides and tangents baked into the syntax. For instance, the opening line is, "He was an angry man, and he was an ugly man, and he was tall, and he was pacing." It's a voice with an edge, one that would be tedious coming from a lesser writer, but you can tell by reading Attenberg that she has written thousands upon thousands of pages. There's a hard-earned fluidness to the prose.

Another thing Attenberg does is glide the point of view into tangential characters. For instance, in one scene Twyla goes to a drug store to buy makeup, and then changes her mind and leaves the makeup on the counter for the clerk to restock. Attenberg goes into the clerk's mind for a couple of paragraphs, and we hear the clerk grumble about Twyla; the clerk tells herself she's getting out and won't be in this dead-end job for long. After this short aside, the book returns to one of the main characters. Point of view shifts like that are a basic no-no in a beginning writers workshop, so why does Attenberg do it? The novel would work fine if she'd followed the "rules," but the shifts in perspective add a shade of something off-kilter to the novel. It gets us out of the heads of the main family and shows a larger, interconnected world. It's an artistic imperfection that makes the book strange and interesting.

You can certainly point to early-career novelists who have deft plots and supple prose (for instance, Lisa Halliday's debut novel *Asymmetry* is one of the best novels I've read in recent years; I also preferred Celeste Ng's debut *Everything I Never Told You* to her second novel, *Little Fires Everywhere*), but when you read a good artist's oeuvre, you witness how they shake off their early influences and step into their own. There's often an expansiveness of vision that accompanies this growth, so it makes perfect sense to me that a novelist's "big" book is usually the third, fourth, or fifth effort: Philip Roth's *Portnoy's Complaint* (fourth book), Ann Patchett's *Bel Canto* (fourth book), Jonathan Franzen's *The Corrections* (third book), Toni Morrison's *Song of Solomon* (third book) and *Beloved* (fifth book), Emily St. John Mandel's *Station Eleven* (fourth book).

Mandel is an interesting case, because I think you see in her the convergence of craft and commercial success. Her first three novels were published by Unbridled, a very good small press. They were well received critically but seemed to have been beneath the radar. Then, when Knopf published *Station Eleven*, Mandel took off. *Everybody* loved that novel, and you can tell by her prose that she has mastered her craft. Again, there's a fluidness to the way she handles scene, and pacing, and time, which you don't quite see in her first three novels. She's loosened up as a writer. Craft-wise, she's at the top of her game, but when it comes to commerce, I suspect her breakout success was aided by having three critically popular books under her belt. They might not have sold well, but she'd had years for reviewers and booksellers and librarians to get to know her. She likely had a few passionate advocates, so when Knopf came in with a strong marketing push for her fourth novel, she likely had the name recognition within the book trade and a strong base of readers ready for her next book.

Mandel's career is the goal. I think most aspiring novelists want a home, a publisher who will stand by them and mentor them through multiple books, so that when you hit the right book at the right time, the pump is primed for success. Unfortunately, that kind of runway is severely lacking in today's publishing world.

At some point in your apprenticeship, you have to start thinking about what kind of life you want. Where you want to live, how you want to spend your days, and where the money is going to come from. You can mentally prepare for ten years of writing in the cold, but as you move through your twenties, away from college or an MFA program, you'll find some of your peers are starting to do well for themselves. They're dressing nicer, driving expensive cars, buying houses. At cocktail parties, people suddenly start talking about home values and the stock market. Company earnings. Brands. *Wall Street Journal* type stuff.

When I moved to Richmond after graduate school, my wife-to-be owned a townhouse in the suburbs. From 2009 when I started work at the newspaper and then got married, to 2014 when my first novel came out, we were living a pretty dull life by memoir standards. I worked inside a corporation, wore khaki pants and a collared shirt tucked in. I watered the lawn. I talked with the neighbors about the foreclosures in our community. I became the president of the HOA.

Some of the writers I knew were living more adventure-some lives. One of my best friends earned a Master of Divinity from Yale, seemingly on a lark, and has traveled extensively to Colombia, Mexico, Ukraine. College friends were in Brooklyn or Queens, gadflying around New York, working for literary agencies or as publicists or starting magazines. Grad school pals were fellowship-hopping around the country. By comparison, my life in the suburbs was tame and decidedly un-literary. No one at the newspaper seemed to care about literary journals, and then I started freelancing, working for ad agencies and big corporations, where *story* refers to the consumer experience and *brands* require character development. Even to this day I cling to Flaubert's notion that it was okay to live like a bourgeois, that it might allow me to be "violent and original" in my work, and I feel like something of a spy, living a double life with my head in the world of the imagination and my employment in the realm of corporate America. I also think about James Dickey's quip about working in advertising while trying to make it as a poet. He said something to the effect of, "I spent my days selling my soul to the devil and my nights trying to buy it back."

One of my professors once compared the aesthetic philosophies of the poets William Carlos Williams and Wallace Stevens. Williams was a doctor who delivered babies, and he summed up his poetic philosophy as "no ideas but in things." He loved the world as it was—the red wheelbarrow and the plums in the freezer—and wanted to express the world in his poetry. Just what you'd expect from someone whose day job involved saving babies. Stevens, meanwhile, worked in insurance, and wrote poetry of the imagination, "the palm at the end of the mind." He investigated being and notions of consciousness, the stuff going on inside his brain. Just what you'd expect from someone whose day job involved analyzing numbers for a product that no consumer who buys it ever hopes to use it.

James Baldwin again: "People pay for what they do, and still more for what they have allowed themselves to become, and they pay for it very simply: by the lives they lead."

In more than one Hercule Poirot story, Agatha Christie cites a Spanish proverb: "Take what you want and pay for it, says God."

To live the life of the mind, you might have to forego material comforts. If you want bourgeois American comforts, perhaps including a family, you may have to sacrifice the time you spend on your art. There's always a cost, and the cost grows as you get older. At some point, you'll need health insurance. You might want to buy a house. You might want to get married, and have children, and live a life. You can knock around for a few years when you're young, but at some point, the lifestyle of "starving artist" will get old, and you'll probably commit to some kind of work.

I can't advise on when that decision will happen, or whether it's worth trying to stick it out until a publication or a teaching job comes through. I suspect the decision won't be a conscious one. It'll merely happen for you, the same way it happened for me. Recently, I mentioned to Emily how bemusing it was that so many of our old friends either went to law school or landed in marketing by middle age, and she replied, "We all grew up."

The question is, how do you keep writing, and how do you keep prioritizing the work of being a novelist, even as you grow up?

5. Enjoy Your First Taste
of Success

Publish your screaming second novel with a reputable small press. Go on book tour. Spend all your earnings on gas and drinks for your true friends who come out to your readings. Try not to get discouraged when it seems like every other novelist is getting more money, making more sales, getting calls from Hollywood. You're on your way. Dream big when a fancy agent emails you to say he wants to rep your next book. Keep working on those next three novels. It's okay that you don't live in Brooklyn.

The nice thing, if *nice* is the right word, about growing up as a novelist is that your material gets a little deeper. Life gets a little messier, and seems more fraught. In late 2011, I quit my job at the newspaper to become a freelance copywriter, thinking that I would eventually get laid off at the paper and I might do better to be in business for myself. After all, I couldn't lay myself off. It took 800 cold calls (I know, because I kept a tally on my wall, twenty calls a day, five days a week, for eight weeks) to get enough freelance business to replace my salary at the paper (admittedly a low bar).

That summer, Emily and I went to California for a wedding for a grad school pal. On the way out of town, the front-page news in Richmond was of a 19-year-old girl who had been killed in a hit-and-run while riding her bicycle home from work one evening. In Los Angeles, my friend had a bachelor's party that involved riding around all night in a limousine, living it up, and I got back to the hotel around four in the morning. I logged into Facebook and saw that the morning's *Times-Dispatch*— 7 a.m. in Richmond—had a story about the alleged culprit in the hit-and-run, a guy I used to work with at the paper. I went to bed stunned by the news, and over the next few days checked in on the commentary back home. The story was sad, and messy, and I immediately began writing about it, but found myself immedi- ately stuck—a personal story without an easy way in. I couldn't square the guy I'd known with the villain in the news. The project would later become my novel *The Merciful*, but in fall 2012 it was one more in a pile of novels stacking up on my hard drive.

I have a hard time remembering my state of mind in late 2012. I turned 30 that fall and had given two novels my all. I was revising a third and had a few more in the drawer, but I was also building a freelance copywriting business and was seeing what the life cycle of such a business might be. Freelancers often start out working for advertising or marketing agencies, whose job is to sell services to big corporations and retain contractors (or young employees) to do the work. As one of the drug dealers on *The Wire* says, "Buy for a nickel, sell for a dime." In the case of a marketing agency, you're buying and selling labor. Eventu- ally, freelance writers, designers, coders, and the like get enough experience and perhaps a few of their own corporate clients, and they start raising their rates. There then comes a moment where *they* have to hire someone for support. The freelancer becomes the businessperson, and over a few years they end up building an agency of their own.

In 2012 I had no interest in building my own agency. I only wanted to make a modest living so I could build a literary career, but I suspect that, if my first novel hadn't been accepted when it was, I would eventually have let the paying work take over and let the creative work fall away. But, in late 2012, I got word from the editor at Hub City Press that she wanted to publish *The Whiskey Baron*, and just like that, my career was off and running. I spent 2013 revising the novel and rewriting *The Edge of America* and gearing up for 2014 promotions.

Here, there is an element of unspeakable luck. I'd known Hub City Press as a consumer, had been reading their books for years, but I didn't know anything about the back end of the industry, and what set Hub City apart from many other independent presses. Chief among them are nice design, good distribution, and connection to the indie bookselling community. If a book doesn't look nice, people won't buy it. If you can't get it into the official "book trade," booksellers won't carry it. If you don't have the personal relationships, no one in the industry will pay attention. Now that I am a publisher myself, I find it confounding how difficult it is to get a book noticed.

Luckily for me, *The Whiskey Baron* received excellent reviews from *Publishers Weekly*, *Library Journal*, and *Kirkus*, three of the big "pre-publication" review journals, which helped get the book into stores and libraries. What's more, after the *Publishers Weekly* review came out, I received an inquiry about the French rights, and we sold the book to Albin Michel for translation and publication in France. An agent from a Very Good Agency emailed me to ask if I had representation, and he eventually took on *The Edge of America*.

This is what you want: the dazzling debut novel experience.

In an essay called "My Life in Sales," Ann Patchett said that the only thing worse than going on book tour is not going on book tour. In 2014, I burned up the highway visiting independent bookstores on the theory that they would be my key to success. The South has long had a vibrant bookseller community, and those early experiences of lurking in the stacks at the Clemson Newsstand had made being a novelist feel like a worthwhile profession. I'd read a profile of Emma Straub in *Poets & Writers*, where she cited strong support from indie booksellers as being the key to the success of her first book, a collection of stories she published with an independent press. On book tour, she made friends with booksellers, sold a modest but respectable number of copies, and moved on to a New York press. Hers was a path one seemingly could follow from the provinces of Virginia, and my plan was to hit up as many independent bookstores as I could on book tour. I'd rack up enough sales to interest a bigger publisher for my second novel, and I'd be on my way.

Key point: You can look for models in this business, but everyone is on their own unique path. What worked for someone else might not work for you. Straub, for instance, is the daughter of bestselling novelist Peter Straub, and she lives in Brooklyn amid the publishing army. Her business model involved more than just her book tour.

My own book tour was fine, if a little demeaning at times. What happens is you show up at a store in some city where you maybe know one person. Maybe that person comes out, and you stand there awkwardly debating whether to make it a formal reading or just to sign their book (which they feel obligated to buy) and call it a day. If a second person comes out, you have to give the reading. At one of my first bookstore events, I took two friends out to lunch, and then we went to the bookstore, where the clerk was the only other member of the audience. I then read a chapter of the book to my two friends I'd just shared tacos with, chatted with the clerk about his own forthcoming book, signed stock, and drove home.

A word about stock: When you do a book reading, the store orders maybe a dozen copies of your book. You might only sell a few copies at the event, but then, in a perfect world, you sign the rest and the bookstore puts them on some prominent display, allowing you to sell ten more books over the next week. The idea—at least in 2014—was that it wasn't about the reading itself, but about making friends with booksellers who would "hand sell" your book after you left. In theory. That may have been true to a certain extent in 2014, but it is much less true today. Even if the theory holds—that you go on book tour, sign a bunch of books, and make allies with booksellers who will be your champions—it is still miserable to show up in some random city where absolutely no one comes out to your event.

After a few weeks on the road, store after store after store after store, my last stop was somewhere in North Carolina. I showed up at the store, and they had set me up in a café area. They'd arranged chairs and made a stack of my books, and the clerk walked me back there and said, quite cheerily, "Here you are!" and then she returned to the front of the store. I stood there by the stool and the stack of my books and looked around. One lady sat at a nearby table, reading a book and eating a salad. Across the room, a couple of teenagers were making out on a couch. No one was here for a reading, and I had a nearly four-hour drive home, and I'd had enough of being on the road. I went up front, signed a few copies, and headed back to Richmond. Somewhere across the Virginia border, exhausted, I started seeing phantom deer in the highway. I pulled over and sort of twitched while curled up against the door for a while.

That's book tour. Patchett was right; the only thing worse would be not going on book tour.

6. Take a Clear-Eyed Look at New York Publishing

It's not okay that you don't live in Brooklyn. It's also not okay that you already have a published novel. The big New York publishers are seemingly only interested in debut novels, preferably from authors who schmooze in Brooklyn. If you write "southern" fiction and want success in New York, it better be in the "methalachia" vein—the great Appalachian meth novel. Realize you are not going to find success in New York.

In the early 2000s, Michael Chabon started ranting publicly in favor of genre fiction. He grumbled about the "contemporary, quotidian, plotless, moment-of-truth revelatory short story," and by 2005, when he guest edited the *Best American Short Stories* anthology, he was in full campaign mode to bring genre fiction out of the ghettos of grocery store paperbacks and into the discourse of contemporary American literature. His efforts had a liberating effect on a number of younger writers who had read our share of horror or crime or mystery or science fiction in our youth—and the late 2000s and early 2010s saw a number of genre-bending literary novels in the mainstream. In addition to Chabon's own experiments with genre, the period saw the publication of Justin Cronin's vampire trilogy, Colson Whitehead's zombie novel *Zone One*, and countless "literary crime" novels. Every genre but romance, it seemed, was experimental ground for literary writers (like Rodney Dangerfield, romance novels never get any respect).

Meanwhile, books that might have been categorized as "genre" in a different era were viewed as the literary fiction of the day. Gillian Flynn's *Gone Girl*, for instance: literary agents on Twitter were citing this straight-up thriller as an example of the type of "literary fiction" they were interested in.

By the time my first novel was released in 2014, the movement Chabon started had peaked. The years from 2013 to 2015 were littered with public handwringing over the difference between genre and literary fiction, and whether there was a difference, or should be a difference. I like that space in between, the ambiguity of an un-classifiable book, but by the time my agent started sending my Florida crime novel, *The Edge of America*, out, the pendulum was shifting. After maybe a year of submissions and enough rejections to call the book dead, he sheepishly said he thought the book was "caught between two chairs—too literary for the genre presses, but too much story to fit in with the slow and plodding literary novels." Set in Miami 1984, the book is about a businessman with CIA ties who gets involved in an ill-advised money laundering operation, and then his teenage daughter steals $3 million out of a safe in his house. There's plenty of story, but I would classify it as a "literary thriller" because it's more than a sequence of suspenseful actions (I think). There are some ruminations, particularly in the first third, that likely make it too slow for the tired reader who could otherwise be binge-watching *Ozark* or *The Americans*.

In other words, the book has some flaws, but they're flaws I appreciated in fiction at the time I wrote the book, and I think it had the unfortunate fate of hitting the market a few years past the peak of what might have been called "crossover fiction"— literary novels with genre-style plots, or genre novels with literary-quality writing. Since about 2014, the genre lines have solidified again, so much that on a recent panel of mystery writers, my co-panelists described their "lanes"—the box their publishers expected them to stay in. When it came my turn to speak on the panel, I had to chime in and say I felt like I was working in a sandbox. A grit-lit-southern-country-noir with *The Whiskey Baron*, and then a South Florida noir-spy novel with *The Edge of America*, and then a meta-fictive trial novel in the pipeline. It occurred to me, while sitting on that mystery panel, that I would probably have a more successful career if I could commit to a publishing lane.

One genre I've long felt ambivalent about is "Southern fiction," a genre I contend died with Larry Brown in 2004. America has always had a richly regional literature, going back to Mark Twain and Sarah Orne Jewett and Charles W. Chesnutt. Why then is "Southern fiction" such a well-defined genre? Why has "Midwestern fiction" not taken off in the same way? After all, it was the Midwesterner Sherwood Anderson who encouraged William Faulkner to tap into the region and make use of his "postage stamp" of the world. Why the South?

One answer might be cultural: arguably the "South" has historically shared a common culture going back to the Confederacy, so that someone in Richmond, Virginia, had a stronger connection with someone a thousand miles away in Jackson, Mississippi—both states formerly of the Confederacy—than with someone 250 miles away in Philadelphia, or even 150 miles away in Baltimore. The South had a shared culture of slavery and defeat, a culture of sweet tea and *y'all* and right-to-work employment. This shared culture gave rise to a shared literature, and the literature was codified in the 1920s thanks to Robert Penn Warren, John Crowe Ransom, and other "fugitive poets" who formed a critical school out of Vanderbilt. Had Sherwood Anderson, Theodore Dreiser, and Sinclair Lewis formed a similar school out of, say, the University of Michigan—the "Midwestern Fugitives," or perhaps the "Midwestern Reticents"—there might be an equally strong genre of Midwestern literature today to rival that of the South.

Over the 20th century, American literature at large became institutionalized inside academia, and by the time Larry Brown was publishing in the 1980s and 1990s, Southern literature had become an almost self-conscious mode, with each generation looking back. I had to go back two generations, to my grandparents' era in the 1930s, to find an authentic "Rough South" to write about in *The Whiskey Baron*, a novel consciously written in the shadow of Faulkner and Cormac McCarthy. In some ways, fiction, like all stories, is about building community, or connecting a community, or connecting to your community. In the 21st century, we've become community-less, which might explain why so many writers are looking back, trying to find something lost.

But what about today? What is happening in the South now? Is there a contemporary "Southern literature"? The majority of Brown's fiction was published by Algonquin, a publishing house based in Chapel Hill, North Carolina, which under the editorship of Shannon Ravenel was a vanguard of Southern fiction. From 1986 to 2010, Algonquin ran an anthology called *New Stories from the South*, which tried to explore and define Southern fiction and a changing South—and it serves as a kind of who's who of Southern writers over the years. In those pages, you can see the changing of the guard, the shift from primarily white writers working in a clearly defined lane, to a multicultural pastiche of writers connected only by the sheer coincidence of geography. By 2010, the South was no longer some single entity with a shared culture going back to the Confederacy. Rather, it was a dynamic place with much in common with the rest of America. I've lived in Richmond since 2008, and I can tell you that although I might be fond of Mississippi, Richmond today feels as much like a D.C. suburb or even Boston than it does Jackson or New Orleans.

What changed? Social media and the mobility of the Millennial generation might have been two death knells for the Old South. Brown was able to write authentically about people who spoke with a twang, lived in the same town they were born in, and were at the mercy of the mill boss. Can any Millennial writer who tries to write like Brown claim authenticity? So much has changed over the past twenty years. My generation grew up with cable television, and people of nearly every economic background are on Facebook today. To write about the South in the 21st century is to write about a place wired up and plugged into the rest of the country. Local culture exists in pockets for sure, but the story of *my grandma on the mountain* often feels like construct, akin to a Pottery Barn dining room table made out of reclaimed barn wood. People still say *ain't* and *y'all*, but they know they're

49

regional terms that serve as markers of identity. A writer today using the word *ain't* makes me think of the hipster opening a Southern biscuit joint, using a recipe he had to hunt down from somebody's grandmother because, more than likely, he grew up eating Pop-Tarts. It's all an attempt to connect with a community of the past.

Here, I'm not trying to deny the importance of *place* in fiction, which is as powerful as ever. I'm also fully aware that regional dialects still exist, and that there's still an authentic sound to working-class work, and that the economic divide in this country may be as wide as it's ever been. Most writers, however, operate in a world of intellectual privilege, and going to college is a bit like leaving Plato's cave. As Thomas Wolfe observed decades ago, you can't go home again. (One irony today is that an MFA graduate working as an early or even mid-career college lecturer might be struggling financially more than your average "Rough South" factory worker.)

What I'm trying to say is that "Southern fiction," as a school of literature, has transformed from a tribe of writers trying to capture a place, into a mode whereby writers are operating in a genre, same as if they set out to write a ghost story or a western. In perhaps a nod to this new reality, Tom Franklin's novels might be read as westerns set in the South—"southerns," perhaps. Like the disconnect between the western genre and life in the West today, the Southern mode is somewhat disconnected from the reality of life in the South. A book set in the South today may or may not fit in the Southern mode. For instance, Colson Whitehead's *The Underground Railroad* is a magic realist slave narrative set in the Antebellum South. This novel wasn't marketed with phrases like "powerful new novel in the Southern tradition." If anything, the novel takes an ax to the "Southern tradition."

Location is divorced from mode. The mode of Southern fiction used to be about place, but now, I'm arguing, Southern fiction is about an idea. Some writer friends and I sometimes talk about "methalachia," thanks to the prominence of Appalachian novels tackling the social ills of meth addiction—or, by 2018, the opioid crisis. This mode started around 2005 or 2006, shortly after Brown passed away. In the mid-2000s, Daniel Woodrell popularized the meth story in *Winter's Bone*, Ron Rash captured it in several short stories, and William Gay wrote what I think is the best piece in this mode, a story called "Where Will You Go When Your Skin Cannot Contain You?" Woodrell, Rash, and Gay were writing about the reality of life as they were seeing it, an emerging evil in rural America in the early 2000s. There followed an onslaught of such fiction, as well as the TV series *Breaking Bad*. In the 2010s, the story of meth in America—and, more recently, opioids—became commodified as an entertainment, as popular in Appalachian fiction today as "haints" and "my grandma on the mountain."

Art (an expression of the self in reality) has become artifice (a consumer product).

Here, I'm really wrestling with my own material. As an author, I come from the Southern tradition, so I've been mulling for years over what the genre is, how it works, and its place in our culture. You likely have your own tradition that you may need to grapple with. This is akin to what T.S. Eliot discussed in his essay "Tradition and the Individual Talent," his idea being that when you write something, there is a long tradition behind you, and you are adding the next link in the chain. The artist can't escape the tradition, but somehow has to work through it to find something new to say, and in so doing the artist effectively changes the past. In Eliot's view—a view I share—you have to understand the context of history, all that came before leading to this moment, in order to express the truth for today.

I'm not sure how relevant this idea is for readers and writers today, in the 2020s. We're living in a distressingly ahistorical period, in which "truth" is not grounded in fact, much less history. It's an Orwellian world: a politician can tweet one thing in the morning, and a complete contradiction in the afternoon, and although plenty of people will call out the contradiction (or the hypocrisy), the politician's supporters never waver. Eliot's vision of the individual talent absorbing and reimagining and adding to a line of tradition sounds absurd in our new post-truth era. It's also, I would argue, one reason why fiction still matters. In some ways, the truth-seeking novelist today is like a medieval monk, preserving history and truth in a dark age, hoping some future reader will come along to carry the torch.

What is the point of aspiring to art if there's no one who can understand where you're coming from? Why bother to publish in the first place? These are unanswerable questions, but at some point, if you want to be a published novelist, you will have to confront your audience and your relationship with them. Are you there to entertain them? Educate them? Are you writing for the masses who want a story at the end of the day? Or a select few who will pick up the most obscure things you put down on the page?

I have no answers for you, but it's been my experience that although you may sit around thinking deeply about genre, or literary history, or history at large, your audience may not have a clue what you are wrestling with. One of the first rules of rhetoric is to consider audience and genre. With my institutionalized MFA background, I'd thought long and hard about genre, but had somehow forgotten there was an audience on the other end. Once, around 2010 or so, I was bemoaning my travails to an older novelist friend, and he suggested I should just email my book to an editor who said he was closed for submissions. I said I worried that was improper, and my friend said, "You're writing for readers, aren't you?" His point was that to get my book out to readers, I needed to be a little bolder, but what struck me was the concept of readers. *Was* I writing for readers? Who or what was I writing for anyway?

I can tell you that with *The Whiskey Baron*, the feedback from readers that meant the most was from everyday people—community college students in small-town South Carolina, for instance, or an aunt who found comfort in the book while going through chemo treatments. Your everyman (or everywoman) reader will pick up what you're putting down, so long as you're clear, but they also don't necessarily have the background in whatever genre or field you've been researching. Balancing those two things—what you know and are trying to express, with the desires and needs of readers—is no easy task, and where you fall on that dividing line could mean the difference between obscurity and bestsellerdom.

As a novelist, you, too, will have to explore and wrestle with your own material. When you start writing, you have literary heroes working in some kind of mode—in my case it was Southern fiction, but it could just as easily have been the mystery genre, or horror, or westerns. In your apprenticeship, you would be well served to understand your mode inside and out, but at some point, the way a teenager shakes off the ideologies of her parents and comes into her own as a human being, you will have to shake off your tradition to find your own individual voice.

Make it new. This was Ezra Pound's advice for artists, and this advice makes it difficult to join a publishing lane. You can get trapped into writing the same thing over and over again. There's a reason Arthur Conan Doyle tried to kill of Sherlock Holmes— and then had to bring him back when his readers revolted. This dynamic is captured nicely in Wilton Barnhardt's novel *Lookaway, Lookaway*, an expose of Charlotte society. In it, a novelist has found success writing Civil War romances, books he despises but must keep writing for the money. It drives him to drink, which leads to hilarity in the novel.

The phenomenon I'm describing is nothing new. If a novelist is lucky enough to conjure lightning in a bottle, eventually she'll be asked to repeat that formula again and again. What is new is that we live in the era of the Personal Brand. We're all Instagram models to some degree, crafting our own presentation. Because of the noise in the marketplace, there is some pressure to become a character to stand out. That's how Donald Trump won the presidency. The challenge of putting on a persona as a character is that, eventually, you either have to strip away the persona to confront the real, or you risk becoming the persona. The example of Ernest Hemingway is probably American literature's most famous case. His early work may be brilliant, but by the time he became "Papa Hemingway," he was writing self-parody, which was largely drivel.

Then you read his posthumous works—*The Garden of Eden* and *Islands in the Stream*—and you see flashes of the real Hemingway, the artist behind the persona.

Earlier, I mentioned the joy of reading an author at the top of her game. That only works if the author doesn't become a caricature. One great challenge for the would-be novelist today, then, is how do you break through the noise, how do you commit to a genre lane, while still pushing yourself artistically? You have to meet your audience where they are, while still trying to do something original. I don't know how you solve that conundrum except to suggest that if you want to write well, you'll need to brace yourself for a long slow start to your career, and possibly a life of obscurity.

7. Consider Having Children

Maybe read Bill McKibben's Falter *first. Children are absolutely wonderful, but it's irresponsible to bring one into this world if you don't understand the concepts of "wet bulb temperatures," "carbon parts per million," and the "singularity." Your children have some tough skating in front of them. Your generation does, too, by the way.*

The singularity is near. Perhaps nothing has influenced my thinking in adulthood as the concept of the tech singularity, popularized by the futurist Ray Kurzweil. The idea is that technology has been accelerating at an exponential rate, and when you look at an exponential graph, the line eventually shoots up to be nearly vertical. We will eventually hit that moment, a singularity, where we cannot fathom what will be on the other side. Thanks to phenomenon known as Moore's Law, computer processing power is doubling every few years, and technology is saturating more and more aspects of our lives. We're experiencing exponential change, and the question is, when will the singularity—that vertical line of unfathomability—arrive?

Exponential growth is difficult to imagine, but most futurists, even if they are bearish on artificial intelligence, seem to think we are in the midst of an acceleration, and that the acceleration will continue for the foreseeable future. There is a famous pair of photographs, one taken in 1903 and one in 1913, of a street corner in New York. The 1903 photograph shows a dirt road with horses and buggies. The 1913 photograph shows a recognizably

modern street taken over by automobiles. Ten years, and everything changed. The current business buzzwords are "disruption"
and "transformation." Blockbuster Video gave way to Netflix;
taxis gave way to Lyft; cameras gave away to smart phones. Every
industry is about to undergo a radical change as we go into the
2020s, and assuming the human species survives, and assuming
future historians one day write about the 2010s and 2020s, they
will cite ours as an era of unprecedented change, an inflection
point in the history of humanity, politics, business.

Will we discover some type of gene therapy that reverses
aging and allows us to achieve immortality? Will artificial intelligence take over the world? Will we embed chips into our brains
so that we become, in effect, something more than human? Or
will we stumble onto a technology so powerful we simply blow
ourselves up?

I can't remember exactly when I first learned about the
concept of the singularity, but I do remember seeing how it was
plausible, and then probable, and feeling an overwhelming sense
of grief for humanity over what we were about to do to ourselves.
The changes are already happening, by degrees. Remember
Gibson's quote: "The future is already here—it's just not very
evenly distributed." And we are going to continue allowing the
changes to happen, I believe. After all, who among us would want
to live in the past, once you considered the true reality of the
past as a dirty, stinky, disease-ridden, dangerous, and if nothing
else *bland* place. I know I certainly want all the latest advances
modern medicine has to offer. And who among us is foregoing all
the advantages of Wi-Fi, smart phones, GPS navigation, instant
messaging services, FaceTime? The Fitbit may have been a fad,
but wearable tech is just the beginning. Implantable tech is on the
horizon, which will continue to change who we are as a species,
same as the smart phones we constantly check for notifications.

Why discuss this in a memoir about becoming a novelist? You
can't divorce art from history; history is about humanity, and art is
an expression of humanity. Where humans go, so goes art. Philip
Roth once said something to the effect of all serious fiction must
eventually confront the issue of consciousness. Consciousness, as

I'll elaborate in a later chapter on point of view, is the inner voice of self-awareness. It's what makes you, you, and it's what defines your characters. The one saving grace in all my reading about the singularity is that no matter how many advancements we see in AI and machine learning, no matter how much tech intrudes in our lives, no one—not the neuroscientists, or the psychiatrists, or the philosophers—have solved the "hard problem of conscious-ness," the question of where this self-aware voice comes from. The human brain is still a complex mystery, but I worry that if we ever do solve that problem, "the human game"—to use the nomenclature of environmentalist Bill McKibben—will be over.

Once we reduce humanity to the level of an operating system, choice—freedom—will no longer exist. Everything will be a pre-determined sequence of code, and novelists will have nothing left to write about. These are issues every thinking novelist must confront in the 21st century—and confront as starkly as you can bear—because confronting the truth is the only pathway to art.

One of the dirty little secrets of publishing is that agents face as much rejection as writers. They take on books all the time that don't sell. While I was on tour for *The Whiskey Baron* in 2014 and 2015, the agent and I worked on revisions to *The Edge of America*. We went through three or four drafts, some them major over-hauls, but he finally felt like it was ready. Something he could sell. Around the time my first daughter was born, he began sending it out to New York.

A year went by: a blur of all the things that come with a child. It's impossible to overstate how much children will change your life—or at least, how much they changed my life. Big-picture, having children cut a deep groove in my soul, almost instantly. But the significant effects happened day to day. You expect the lack of sleep for a few months. You expect the diapers. You expect the worry over finances. One thing I expected but was still caught off guard by is how relentless parenthood is. Your time is no longer your own.

Lucy Ellmann, author of *Ducks, Newburyport*, caught some flak on Twitter for saying in an interview that having children in a climate emergency might be ill-advised, and that motherhood takes its toll on women who could otherwise be productive members of society. She told *The Guardian*, "People don't talk enough about how tiring, boring, enraging, time-consuming, expensive and thankless parenthood is." Her capper, the line everyone took the most issue with, was: "You watch people get pregnant and know they'll be intellectually and emotionally absent for 20 years. Thought, knowledge, adult conversation and vital political action are all put on hold while this needless perpetuation of the species is prioritized."

Ellmann is a parent herself and knows whereof she speaks. I think parenthood is more joyful than she lets on in that passage, but those comments ring true to me as a father. Motherhood certainly takes more of a toll than fatherhood, no matter how engaged Dad is. Yet fathers too experience the fatigue, the boredom, the loss of time and money. With one baby, you can trade off with your spouse, but once the second baby arrives, you don't just go to the movies. You don't binge-watch the latest show. You don't knock on doors for a political campaign. You don't meet your pals at the bar. Instead, you wash dishes. You try to keep up with your email while on the toilet. You watch your face sag and your hair grow gray. You're under fire, and you disappear from the world for a while. In that time, your priorities also change, and becoming a novelist may no longer matter. That's okay, too.

There is a moment with one child, when you get her sleeping through the nights, where she will sleep twelve hours at a clip. You have about a year of respite before the terrible twos kick in and you, for some reason, start thinking about a second kid. In that period of respite with our first daughter, I finally sat down and drafted *The Merciful*, about the hit and run, four years after the event in Richmond. I set it on the South Carolina coast and employed a structure along the lines of the film *Rashomon*, four novellas circling around the incident and the subsequent trial from different perspectives, all linked by a frame narrator. What I'm most proud of in this structure is that it gave me a way to explore four separate consciousnesses. One character works for a data analytics company, and is confronting the survival of humanity—those issues I started this chapter with. The character's work leads him into the world of brain emulations and simulated reality—apt, given that the story is a simulated reality within the frame narrator's mind.

It's not a perfect novel, but I still think it is the best piece of fiction I'll ever produce. It came out of me in a way that felt transcribed, like it came through me. I don't ascribe to a whole lot of woo-woo commentary around writing—for instance, I don't believe authors who say, *Oh my characters started talking to me*, or, more precisely, I think they're delusional hams—but something came over me, working on that book while my daughter slept in the next room. That's what I meant when I said a moment ago that children cut a deep groove in my soul. Suddenly, my life was no longer my own; my wife and I were responsible for another life that will, barring catastrophe, outlive us and carry on in the world. The future of the world—and the true nature of the world—were suddenly more than dispassionate curiosities, but existential threats. What was I doing having a child if the human brain was merely an operating system, or if the world around us was a simulation, or if the tech or environmental catastrophe would soon wipe us out? The *merciful* of the title refers to the players in my fictional world who put the man on trial, and is of course a reference to the Beatitudes. *Blessed are the merciful, for they will be shown mercy.* In my view, the inheritors of the world are the ones who need the mercy.

After I finished the novel, I sent it to my agent, who had been keeping me abreast of his progress with *The Edge of America*. The rejections had come in at a steady pace over the year it had been on submission, and although he was still positive, I was already abandoning that novel's prospects. My agent read *The Merciful*. I waited. Then we had The Talk.

The Edge of America was "caught between two chairs," he said, and although he still had some leads for it, he wasn't sure it was going to happen. I could tell he felt terrible, but I'd always admired him for his forthrightness. He was savvy and direct.

And *The Merciful?*

Jon, you've written a lot of words here. Good words. I don't think I'm the guy to sell it. I think I'll run into the same issue.

The direction was clear: I could write another, different novel, or I could shop *The Merciful* elsewhere. I went to the beach with Emily and our daughter. We played in the ocean, and when our daughter was napping, I sat around generally feeling sorry for myself. I thought it over, and when we went home, I broke up with my agent.

Agent break-ups happen all the time, too. You go into this business thinking you want stability—an agent in your corner, a publisher who will support you through multiple books, a Maxwell Perkins-like editor who can tease out your true genius and make you shine. Instead, most writers are on their own at all times.

What can you do? It's a numbers game, and everyone in the industry is trying to eke out a living the best way they can. On Twitter recently, one agent said she received 10,000 queries in 2019 and took on three new clients. I can't find any data about how many projects agents take on eventually sell (or not), but I know it's not 100%. Although I don't have any data to support this, I suspect a good agent has a batting average of 30-50%, meaning one of that agent's three projects for 2019 will sell and the other two might not.

Key point: One out of 10,000 is as good a rule of thumb as any for your odds of selling a novel.

I started querying agents again. I reached back out to some agents who had read *The Whiskey Baron*, and went back and forth with one agent over a few rounds of edits to *The Merciful*, and just when I was starting to think I'd made a terrible mistake—that I needed to go back to Agent #1 and give him a sequel to *The Whiskey Baron*, get in the country-noir lane and write a bunch of novels about a small-town sheriff in the thirties—a new agent offered me representation. Great! But he had edits.

Another year went by, a year of edits and trying for a second kid, and then our second daughter was born and Agent #2 started sending *The Merciful* out to New York editors. Until now, I'd not thought about how I had two books with two agents go out on submission right in sync with the birth of my two daughters. The very month each of my daughters were born, I had a novel go off to New York to die. It's a nice coincidence that was lost on me in the moment, the slurry of months which became years as time accelerated.

I started powerlifting.

Somehow, I wrote another novel, about a newspaper reporter who gets involved in an espionage corruption scandal.

I played with my children. Worked on sharing with our older daughter, worked on sleep training with our younger daughter. I tried not to think about climate change and the ethics of having children given the existential threats facing our species.

I waited for news out of New York.

Agent #2 had a different style from Agent #1. Instead of sending out small batches, waiting, massaging the book, sending out more small batches, et cetera, et cetera, Agent #2 shot-gunned the book out to a dozen presses. Rejections shot-gunned right back to us, which he forwarded along without comment. He sent the book out in September, and by Thanksgiving that first wave of editors had largely passed (or disappeared without replying to my agent, those cretins). I took a look at the rejections in the aggregate, but there wasn't anything useful in the feedback, except it seemed like *The Merciful* was also caught between two chairs. A Very Literary Press editor said she enjoyed it but that the trial in the last third was too plot-driven for her taste. A Somewhat Pulpy Press editor said he could tell I was a good writer but found the opening third too ruminative. I cut out the frame narrator, came up with a pulpier title, and in January 2018 sent it over to Agent #2.

He said he liked the revision and shot-gunned it out to another dozen or so presses. This time, only a few editors replied, and in the process Agent #2 slowly quit the business. He didn't tell me directly what he was doing, but from what I sussed out, he was feeling the same kind of down-in-the-dumps as I was. We'd struck out, so sorry. I was a little pissed at the time but don't begrudge him. An agent specializing in literary fiction is running up against the same dismal wall as the rest of us. On a 15% commission, you need a few hits to stay in business. I can tell you from personal experience that you can't even live next to a meth dealer in Lafayette, Indiana, off a thousand bucks here, a thousand bucks there. An agent needs the fat five-figure advances to earn a living. We're all subject to the cold reality of a free market.

Take what you want and pay for it, God said.

8. Take Up Powerlifting

You're getting older, and your body doesn't spring back like it used to. You need to exercise regularly. Maybe you always rolled your eyes at the bodybuilders in the gym, but there is wisdom in the body as well as the mind. You can achieve that wisdom five reps at a time. Also, the abstract problems of publishing don't mean as much when you have a 200-pound bar on your back. Find a new agent. Find a friend in real estate.

If you want to talk about the making of a novelist, you eventually have to talk about the larger history within which said novelist came of age. Earlier, I cited the CofC English department's focus on close reading as integral training for a writer. This is true; a novelist needs to understand how a text works line by line. But when you write fiction, you are expressing some version of yourself, and the "self," to some extent, is shaped by the culture you live in.

Here, I want to talk about personal history, or rather, history during my personal life. I was born in 1982, in Reagan's America. One of my earliest memories of the news is the space shuttle *Challenger*'s explosion. In elementary school, years later, I would think about what those astronauts would have experienced. I would look at photographs of the explosion and wonder if they were conscious all the way down. I can't help but wonder now if this early impression has made me skeptical of technology, always looking for the worst-case scenario. Reagan said of the disaster, "Sometimes, when we reach for the stars, we fall short."

I don't have much memory of the 1988 election, or the Berlin Wall falling, but I do vividly remember the first Gulf War, watching images on television of U.S. soldiers riding through the desert in tanks, enemy combatants waving white flags. Around that time I became aware of Vietnam, and how we'd failed in that war, and how young men had been drafted against their wishes. I developed a sense of dread that would carry me through several years in the early nineties—fear that we would go back to war in the Middle East and that my father might be drafted, or that I myself might be drafted when I came of age. Like a lot of boys who grew up in the country, I had toy guns and played army in the woods, but part of me wasn't playing. When my neighbors and I would lurk in the woods with our camo clothes and our plastic guns, I was training for the next war.

The next war came, of course, when I was a freshman in college. It's baffling to me that nearly twenty years have passed since 9/11, because that day is still so vivid in my memory, as it is in the memories of everyone who lived through it. I had no connection to New York then, had never been there and didn't even know the World Trade Center was two buildings known as the Twin Towers. All I knew was that Manhattan was an island of skyscrapers, and when I watched the second plane hit the South Tower on television, I knew it was not an accident and that we were experiencing a moment that would be defined as a Before and an After.

I sometimes wonder if those of us in my generation who never served in the War on Terror will one day be accounting for why, the way some Boomer politicians have felt the need to explain why they never served in Vietnam. I doubt it. The wars in Afghanistan and Iraq have been called "the forever wars," but "the forgotten wars" seem more appropriate, given that most of the country seems to have forgotten we still have troops in both countries, nineteen years after 9/11. For myself, I'm not sure it occurred to me to enlist, at least not right away. It didn't take much sifting through the news to understand the lie at the heart of our politicians' response to 9/11: "They hate us because we're free." To someone who traffics in words, those words are meaningless. If there is a coherent rationale, *they*—whoever *they* referred to—hated us because of our foreign policy, our meddling in the Middle East, our support of Israel.

I vaguely remember discussing the military with my father, and have a memory of him suggesting it would be better to finish college first to go in as an officer, if I wanted to do that. By the time I finished college in 2005, I had nothing but contempt for Bush, the Republican party, and the wars they had led us into, and I wasn't about to enlist to serve their cause. It pains me to say this now, because I do have great respect for the military and the veterans I know. I admire their patriotism and their ethic of service, but for myself, I was angry at American leadership in the mid-2000s, and I still have trouble understanding how the country re-elected Bush when, by November 2004, it was clear the administration had manipulated us into a failing and costly war. How could anyone look at the images of torture out of Abu Ghraib—which were published well before the election—and feel like they were voting for a just cause?

Recently, around the time of Trump's election, I was discussing the 2004 election with some business friends in Richmond, and I discovered too late into my ranting that they may have been Bush supporters (although they were staunch Clinton supporters in 2016). I remember one friend shrugging and saying, in 2016, "Well, I guess back then my kids were young and I wasn't paying all that much attention."

Paying attention.

That's the job of the novelist. To be, in Henry James's phrase, "one of the people on whom nothing is lost."

All of that backdrop—9/11 and the War on Terror and the deterioration in Iraq—was going on during my apprenticeship as a writer and continues to inform what I write about. Then came the 2008 Financial Crisis, at a time when I was struggling to get established in life. My wife and I took over the mortgage on her townhouse from her parents, and it promptly dropped in value so that we were twenty grand underwater in the first months of our marriage. I worked for a media company, which was also a large corporation, and although I didn't realize it at the time, in the depths of the Great Recession, I was embarking on twin careers as a novelist and a businessman. Teaching was in my rearview, and I would make my living as a corporate communications consultant (a fancy phrase for "memo writer") while trying to make a go of it as a novelist.

Then came the drone strikes, and the Boston Marathon bombing, and government surveillance, and ISIS, and birtherism, and Black Lives Matter, and #MeToo, and the Syrian refugee crisis, and the election of Donald Trump, and Charlottesville, Ukraine, impeachment, Iran. All things happening around me and impossible to separate from what I put into my novels.

We live in a time when technology is accelerating, yet culture too has been accelerating at an astonishing rate. By temperament, I prefer slow, incremental but lasting change, yet every day there is some new scandal, some new qualification for being "woke," and the new thing, as I write this, is "cancel culture," wherein the Twitter mob comes for you and actively works to get you "cancelled"—i.e., to silence you, get you fired, bury you. These are fraught times that make little sense, day to day. Things have gotten slippery and gray, which is great for being a novelist but also makes you want to hold onto something tangible.

Hence, powerlifting.

What follows in the rest of this chapter has little to do with being a novelist, but also has everything to do with being a novelist.

I've always been a runner, a solitary thinker who sifts through ideas on a trail, but as I moved through my twenties I became more and more of a fair-weather runner. In winter I would put in the obligatory thirty minutes on a treadmill at the Y, but soon after our first daughter arrived, I started thinking I needed to do more for my health, to try to stay in shape to be a capable father, the hunter-gatherer instinct coming out. I started taking boot-camp and TRX classes at the Y, and this new calisthenics routine worked well for a couple of years.

Around the time my wife was pregnant with our second daughter, one bootcamp instructor had the class doing deadlifts, and I struggled to lift the barbell with 45s—a big plate on either side, 135 pounds total, a good starting weight for deadlifting. Feeling weak, I looked up proper form on the internet and talked to pal I knew who weight-lifted. I found out my friend could deadlift about 400 pounds, which made me feel really weak. I'd stumbled onto a whole new world of fitness.

Most people who decide to take up lifting eventually discover one of two programs, Starting Strength and Strong Lifts 5x5. Both programs have the same general philosophy, which is that heavy weight for five reps is the way to build strength. Trainers in most gyms seem to promote lower weight for higher reps, perhaps out of liability concerns. Barbell training does require good form and some dedicated planning, but it also bring clarity to your gym routine. Low weight with high reps promotes hypertrophy—big muscles. High weight with low weights promotes dense muscles—a.k.a., strength. That was appealing now that I was regularly carrying around a toddler and all her gear.

In addition to sets of five, the introductory lifting programs lean on a principle known as linear progression, or linear progressive overload. The idea is that if you squat a certain weight on Monday, you will stress your muscles enough that they need a couple of days of repair. When you go to squat on Wednesday, your muscles will have strengthened to lift a little more weight than they did on Monday. On Friday, more weight still, and so forth. There's a limit to how far this type of approach can carry you, but most of us are completely untrained and will respond for a few months, and have the potential to get very strong, very fast.

After our second daughter was born, I let my gym membership lapse and set up a squat rack in the garage. My wife soon joined me out there in the evenings, after the kids went to bed, and for a few years now we have been working out together, with a focus on the big three of powerlifting—squats, presses, and deadlifts. We both have hit some general plateaus—I'm nowhere near a 400-pound deadlift like my pal, though I secretly hope to pull that weight around my 40th birthday—but we've both gotten much stronger than we ever have before. The real goal is to stay agile enough so we don't wrench our backs while schlepping our children around. I also want to make sure I go into old age with some solid dense muscle so that when I start to shrink and shrivel like a raisin, I won't break something just from getting out of bed in the morning.

What I like about powerlifting is that it requires focus, and planning, and has measurable results. There's no more futzing around, going to the gym when convenient, and if you do go to the gym, there's no more wandering around, doing a little leg press if the machine is free, and then maybe a few curls ("curls for the girls," a gym rat once joked), and then maybe finish up on the treadmill so you feel like you really got a sweat going. No, with powerlifting you know what you have on tap every day, and how much weight to put on the barbell, and how many reps and sets to do. Then you either lift the weight or you don't. You track your progress over time, and you either lift heavier season by season or you don't.

That kind of objective measurement is in short supply these days. You see it in your workout notebook, week by week. The days you felt a little sniffly and took it easy, or skipped the workout. You see where you were being lazy, and you see, in black and white, the limits of your own body at a given time. Lifting more weight—from 135 to 185 to 225 to 275 to 315 pounds—takes work, hard work, disciplined work. It requires a habit. Three days a week every week for months on end. One hour, three times a week may not seem like much, but maintaining it consistently is where the wheat separates from the chaff.

Of course, this is exactly how novel-writing works. The pages pile up, and you see your progress, in black and white, from one week to the next, one season to the next. At the end of every year, you have an objective accounting of what you have accomplished, or where you've slacked off. You may have real limits—just as I have real limits in the weight room—but you can improve incrementally.

A slow, grind-it-out change.

9. Hit Rock Bottom

Read Richard Rohr's Falling Upward. *Understand the truth of your situation. You have spent the first half of your life building a vessel for your identity, and now the task before you is to fill the vessel up, which is a very different job than the one you were doing. You're 36 years old. Half your friends are on the rocket ship of success, and the other half are struggling mightily. Nothing is how you thought it would be.*

Even at the time—late 2017 and through 2018, when my literary career was approaching what seemed like rock bottom—I felt like I was living through the inspirational montage period of life. I was down and out, but the *Rocky* theme was playing, and I was drinking raw eggs and trying to build up the strength to race up the steps of the Philadelphia art museum at dawn. Or perform a heavier set of squats. Get a third plate onto my deadlift. Write a new novel and find a new agent and achieve fame and fortune. Success was right around the corner. I could feel it.

I am writing this book today at the beginning of 2020, a few months into life as the publisher of Haywire Books. *The Edge of America* is out in the world, and I have a plan to put out several more novels from other authors, as well as *The Merciful*. Things are going as well as could be expected, though sales are about half of what I was hoping for. Was the year from 2017-2018 my montage sequence? Is this what success looks like? At the end of the original *Rocky*, he loses the fight to Apollo Creed, though it's something of a personal victory that he remains upright for the whole fifteen rounds. Like Rocky, my literary career is still standing, if battered.

Here, it might be worth reflecting on friendship for a moment. Friendship among authors is a nuanced thing, and can be edged with competition and petty jealousies in the zero-sum game of publishing. But your fellow authors are also going to be your strongest supporters, and the only people who really know what it's like to be a writer. I've been lucky to find a handful of writer friends over the years, many of whom are also my closest friends in life. These are the people who read my works in progress, and whom I text with every week. They know who they are so I won't embarrass them here, but I will share something a friend from high school once said. He worked for the House of Leung, a now bull-dozed Chinese restaurant in Clemson, which apparently had a great company culture or at least a good group of people working there in the late nineties. One day I was grumbling about some coworkers at my own job, and my friend said, "Who you work with makes all the difference."

I think he was about seventeen at the time, and he likely doesn't remember even saying such an offhand comment, but it's a point lost on many a Vice President of Human Resources. Company culture matters, and the people you work with often, if not always, matter more than the work you do. Peer influence is what keeps an office pleasant (or not), ethical (or not), creative (or not), and productive (or not). Novel-writing is a solitary profession, but the writers you let into your orbit will either lift you up or keep you down. Their philosophies of writing will influence yours, as your philosophy influences theirs. You'll trade book recommendations, maybe spend a year producing an ill-advised podcast together, and discuss everything from the latest political scandal to which fellow writer might be sociopaths to the existence of God. Over time, these conversations will shape who you become as a writer. Not that it's necessarily a choice, but try to find friends who are your kind of people, the people you can sit down at a table with for a drink and remain there for ten hours in good company. Such friends will draw the best out of you.

*

In late 2017, I caught up an old friend from college and graduate school. For years, we'd sent a few annual emails and an exchange of family Christmas cards, but, down in the dumps one week, I emailed to suggest we do a weekly work swap. We'd email each other our work for the week, whatever it was. No commentary necessary, just accountability. I've never been involved in a real writers group or done that kind of accountability measure (and, truthfully, had looked down my nose at them as somewhat weak-willed), but with rejections for *The Merciful* streaming in and no new writing in months, I was fast approaching what felt like the bottom.

This friend and I are still exchanging work; sometimes we'll comment on it; sometimes we'll go a few weeks with nothing but "Welp, no work this week," but I've also written drafts of two novels in two years, a pace I hadn't sustained in nearly a decade. In early 2018, I pulled out some old material I had in a drawer—a big mess of a book that was partly a sequel to *The Whiskey Baron*, partly a story about my grandmother's Connecticut family, and partly a story about a newspaper reporter investigating a dead Cold War spy. I decided to cut out all the past material and brought my newspaper reporter into present-day Charleston, South Carolina. I had him working on two articles—a story about a dead body that had washed up on Folly Beach and an obituary write-up of an old corrupt judge.

Week by week, I sent a chapter or two over to my pal, and week by week I wrote a kind of spy novel in the vein of John Le Carre, a complex web of intrigue and adventure called *The Holy City*. I don't know that I would have written the novel had I not had my pen pal offering encouragement every week. Some writers have talked about writing to a singular reader. For instance, Stephen King has talked about his "Constant Reader." I think having a single reader in mind is helpful, not only because it forces you to think about how many details this one particular reader will need in order to pick up what you're putting down on the page, but it can also keep you from feeling depressed about the pointlessness of your job. If one person wants to read what you're writing, sometimes that's enough.

When I finished and revised and was feeling pretty good about my spy novel, I had an opportunity to talk with an agent about it at my local James River Writers Conference. He and I went out for drinks and talked about the industry at large. We had a great time, but he gave me what I think was the best honest take on the industry that I've gotten from an agent. Essentially, it was simply a miserable time for selling literary fiction. He said his Very Big Agency had had a two-day firm meeting to talk about the market and try to analyze what was going on in the fiction world. The best answer he had for me was Donald Trump, that reality had gotten so surreal that readers were hungry for nonfiction, true stories to ground them in a world swirling with "fake news."

This agent may have been trying to make me feel better, or just talking for the sake of talking, but one true thing I understood was that I had one distinct disadvantage on the market: I'd already had a modest debut book, which meant I was now what is known as a "midlist" writer—"midlist" referring to the spot in the middle of a publisher's catalog. Not the flashy young debut author, and not the bestseller, but someone in the wide middle of obscurity. Remember the concentric rings from the beginning of this book? People on the outside have the advantage of not having had a debut book, and therefore no track record. People in the very center have the advantage of name recognition. The majority of us in the middle are left grinding it out in an increasingly competitive landscape.

This was not news to me in late 2018. I had plenty of novelist friends by this point, many of whom were in exactly the same position. Few people talk openly about this, perhaps because it feels like admitting failure, but authors are constantly being dropped from their publishers, or being told by their agent that their latest project won't sell. People do discuss New York being debut-driven, meaning the focus is on debut fiction at the expense of second or third or fourth novels from midlist authors. If there is a "cult of the debut," it would help explain why the big bestselling books you see on prominent display are either by established writers (i.e., John Grisham and Elizabeth Gilbert) or debut novelists (i.e., Delia Owens).

If I had to guess a reason for this, it would be that debut novels provide a media hook. With your first novel, everybody you know will come out to your book launch and support you. On the road with *The Whiskey Baron*, I ran into so many old friends and even acquaintances from high school, perhaps because knowing a published writer is unusual. Combine the support you get from your personal network with the media's love of potential, and your debut book could break out huge. On tour with *The Edge of America* in 2019, by contrast, almost no one came out to my events. One book is a novelty; two books is a routine.

With this dynamic in mind, it seems like the big publishers' business models involve acquiring a whole lot of debut novels. Most of them will sell 3,000 copies apiece and barely break even on the profit-and-loss statement, but one of them will sell a few hundred thousand copies, get turned into movies, and become a cash cow that subsidizes the rest of the list. I'm not sure it's fair to say New York publishers are completely debut-driven, but I do think it's fair to say they are "book-driven" rather than "author-driven." If you have the right book at the right time, a big press might get behind you, but that doesn't mean anything about your next book. You have no runway to write a bad book, and one whiff of slow sales is a death knell. Although few are discussing this, many of our contemporary authors' careers are in shambles. If you've ever looked at your bookshelf and wondered, "Whatever happened to…," now you know.

The death of the midlist author has been written about for years, but I worry that not only is there an entire generation of us who have been lost in all the industry changes, but soon there might not be a generation of writers with the talent and who have put in the work to write a truly great book. In the business world, a number of industries are worried about knowledge transfer as the older generation retires. For instance, my father recently retired from the nuclear power industry. Power plants tend to be way out in the country, away from urban areas where young engineers want to live. His company was having a hard time attracting and retaining young talent, and when he retired, he was one of the last people who knew how to do his particular type of work. He is a man with a lifelong mistrust of the government and the bureaucratic procedures of the Nuclear Regulatory Commission (NRC), but when he retired he commented that the NRC was probably the one thing standing between the populace and nuclear catastrophe. The industry wasn't making the necessary investments to run properly. For my father to say that, to acknowledge that bureaucratic regulators were the saviors, tells you just how badly the industry is being run.

The stakes in publishing are lower, but I see the same phenomenon at work. The midlist writer is your bench strength, and most of us need a few books to find our material. I think it's important not just to write those books, but to have those books published. Not only can that help you start building an audience, but it can also provide some validation about your career to keep you going. I think there's also something to be said for the way a published book forces you to answer to your readers. Most authors read their reviews, including the ratings on Amazon and Goodreads, and while it can be a disheartening experience, it can also be revealing. You get a sense of who is reading your books and what they got out of them, which I think makes you a better writer. Something happens to you psychologically when you consider the reality of your work being read by strangers. The risk is you might become cautious, out of fear of revealing too much, but I think reviews have pushed me to try to be clearer, more direct.

I once visited a community college with the writer John Lane. The administrators set the two of us in a room where students could come in for a Q&A session on a rolling basis for a few hours. It was a strange experience, because we were getting the same questions every forty-five minutes or so, and our conversation devolved into discussions about the end of the world, the volcano in Yellowstone, and the Anthropocene. Over four hours, I had about five kids ask me why I didn't number the chapters in *The Whiskey Baron*. I have no real answer for that, except to say I kind of liked the sparseness of not having chapter headings. But that bothered the students to no end, and with their questions in mind, I numbered the chapters in *The Edge of America*, simply so I wouldn't have to answer the question again.

*

Perhaps the less said about rock bottom, the better. The lesson in all of this, if there is one, is that if you embark on a career as a novelist, it's impossible to exaggerate what a struggle you are setting yourself up for. In the words of the Steve Miller Band, "time keeps on slippin', slippin', slippin'." If you start young and work hard, there's still a good chance you will be in your thirties before you get a traditional book deal, and most of us can't conceptualize at twenty or twenty-five what that long slog will be like. The years of writing. The tension between your mind and the world around you. The impossibility of publishing. And finally, the folly of this whole endeavor.

In 2018, I was in my montage phase, powerlifting and writing my Charleston spy novel and trying to regroup from having Agent #2 quit on me. Until this point, I'd spent my life trying to understand wisdom from the outside. I'd taken in Bret Lott's philosophy of *I know nothing*. I'd read about failure and overcoming hurdles. I'd read my Richard Rohr, whose book *Falling Upward* is a primer on failure and success in the second half of life. As I slid into my mid-thirties, I was beginning to understand there are some things you can't prepare for. Some things you can't understand without experiencing them firsthand. I'd spent my entire adult life thinking about cultivating humility at my desk, trying to accept the mystery of each novel as it emerged, when it turned out the whole time I was living with a sense of hubris and didn't even know it. I'd thought I *understood* what I was doing, and what was happening around me, and what the point of it all was.

Even now, on the other side of that period, I don't trust anything. We're all floating around in lifeboats, and a wave could swamp us any time. Everything is vanity, everything is folly. Yet I'm still here like Sisyphus, trying to push the rock up the hill one more time. Only now, I feel like I've put a stake in the ground. I've said *screw it* to the forces that be and started Haywire Books to give myself and writers in the same situation a channel. Will it work? Who knows! But today, for the first time in a long while, I feel confident I won't look back and say I didn't give it my all.

10. Throw a Hail Mary

You've committed this far. Take your savings and get ready to push the rock up the hill one more time. Start a small publishing house. Put out your own book. Virginia Woolf did it. Dave Eggers. Kelly Link. You might make it. If not, you're too old for law school, but there's always a career in real estate. (You did make friends with a realtor, right?) Remember: Know thyself. *You'll be fine.*

As we near the end of The Career portion of this book, a recap may be helpful: I started my career by majoring in English and getting an MFA and then looking for teaching jobs. I wrote and wrote and wrote, and eventually started publishing short stories in the literary magazines. I shelved my first novel, but found a small press to publish my second novel, *The Whiskey Baron*, in 2014. Then, over the next five years, two agents couldn't sell two books and a third agent told me I likely wasn't going to find a publisher with my track record and in this dragging market. In late 2018, conscious of my age (35) being the midpoint of the proverbial three score and ten, I decided to start a small publishing house, Haywire Books.

Many things pushed me into this. First, I felt like I had written enough, and written my best, but it wasn't enough. I either wasn't good enough or hadn't gotten lucky enough to break into New York. Second, I was looking at the market and all the changes in publishing, and realized there were some intractable structural barriers stacked against me. Third, I saw I wasn't alone.

I knew many novelists, including a few close friends, who had books languishing on their hard drives because they didn't fit a certain mold.

Finally, after my agent quit, I was shopping *The Merciful* around myself with some small presses. I'd submitted it to LSU for their Yellow Shoe Series, and the editor told me it made it into his final round, but he could only choose one book, and my book wasn't it. The book he chose that year ended up being one of my old literary heroes, George Singleton. After a career of bouncing from Algonquin to New York to Dzanc, Singleton published *Staff Picks* with LSU. That's a great book, and contains at least one story ("Everything's Wild") that is one of my favorite stories he's ever written. I don't know why he landed with LSU, but I suspect he was running into the same thing late in his career that I was in the early part of mine, which is that if you're not in a particular swim lane, doing something in fashion, there's no room for you in New York.

I mentioned a few chapters ago that one of my favorite books in recent years was Steve Yarbrough's *The Unmade World*, published by Unbridled Books. Yarbrough is also late in his career, with a dozen or more books under his belt. He started with the precursor to Unbridled, MacMurray & Beck, in the late nineties, but then published most of his novels with Knopf. I don't know why he left Knopf—perhaps he felt like he would get better editing and a better experience with Unbridled (which I think is one of the very best small presses in business today), but it's possible Yarbrough too had run into the limits of New York and its current publishing model.

In an ideal world, independent presses would be like baseball's farm league, building and sustaining talent until the right book came along—the way Emily St. John Mandel published three books with Unbridled before moving to Knopf with *Station Eleven*. That still happens for some writers, but there aren't enough slots in the small presses to accommodate all the writers. Maybe the answer is we need fewer writers, but in 2018 I chose to see it as a gap in the market. LSU and Unbridled were publishing established masters. West Virginia University Press and the University of Ohio Press rejected *The Merciful* because it wasn't an Appalachian novel. My first publisher, Hub City Press, was still only doing first novels. Meanwhile, Blair and Carolina Wren Press had just merged. When Pat Conroy died in 2016, the University of South Carolina Press dropped his Story River fiction imprint. There just weren't many small or university press options for a non-Appalachian southern novel, so I decided to create one.

My theory about building a career, in an ideal world, is that you need some runway to find your material and build an audience. Maybe the first few novels sell a couple thousand copies apiece, and then you sell ten thousand copies, and then twenty, and then you're a steady, middle-of-the-road seller. In her essay "My Life in Sales," published in *This Is the Story of a Happy Marriage*, Ann Patchett documents this effect at work. On tour for *The Patron Saint of Liars*, she had no audience. With *Taft*, she had a few people come out, mostly people who had read her first novel and wanted an autograph. With *The Magician's Assistant*, she could fill a room, and with *Bel Canto*, she had hundreds of people ready to meet her. She's had an ideal career, but that's how it's supposed to go, if you can find a publisher who will give you the runway for such a take-off.

My favorite story about the disconnect between the runway necessary to build a career and the here-and-now pressures of a publisher's profit-and-loss statement is the career of Ron Rash. He started as a short story writer and poet, and spent decades under the radar. His first five books were published with extremely small presses, and couldn't have sold more than a few hundred copies apiece. His breakout book was his debut novel, *One Foot in Eden*, published when he was in his mid-forties. It won a regional award in Charlotte called the Novello Prize and was published in hardback. Henry Holt picked up the paperback rights and signed him on for two more novels and a book of short stories, which he published in short order over the next five years.

Rash likely had a small, local, but devoted following when *One Foot in Eden* came out, and that novel seems to have drawn a great deal of regional attention to him—attention that was amplified with his next several books. Yet in 2007, Henry Holt dropped him from their list, presumably because the bean counters decided he wasn't selling well enough to issue another contract. I don't know what his sales numbers were, but I believe he was solidly in the midlist, selling somewhere in the five figures, but what no one seemed to be paying attention to was that he was a beloved Appalachian writer who was poised for takeoff. Harper-Collins picked up his fourth novel, *Serena,* which became his best-selling book—a *New York Times* bestseller and an unfortunately bad movie starring Bradley Cooper and Jennifer Lawrence. His imprint, Ecco, did a nice job designing and promoting *Serena,* but they generally have the same distribution and marketing infrastructure as Henry Holt. I suspect either publisher would have seen the same runaway success with the novel, because all the forces had converged for Rash: a great story and an audience hungry for his next novel.

I can point to countless writers whose career followed this kind of arc, but I can also point to writers who never really took off. For instance, William Gay was beloved in the southeast but died before he really hit the big time. Donald Harrington had an entire career of groundbreaking books without becoming a household name. There's an element of luck in publishing, which can cut both ways. The writer Holly Goddard Jones's first novel *The Next Time You See Me,* for example, came out right in the middle of a dispute between her publisher, Simon & Schuster, and Barnes & Noble, which at the time was still one of the most important forces in book sales. Although her novel was critically acclaimed, my sense is that the novel didn't do nearly as well as it could have simply because Barnes & Noble wouldn't stock it.

Then there's plain old *je ne se quoi.* "Some are anointed," the writer James Salter reportedly once said. He was an astonishing writer with an astonishing style, but I don't think he was ever a household name. A critical biographer in the mid-nineties wrote that Salter's bestselling novel was *Solo Faces* (1979), which sold

12,000 copies. His publishing numbers may have changed with the publication of his late-in-life novel, *All That Is*, in 2013, but in this industry there really is no accounting for taste, or for one author taking off while another languishes in the midlist.

Key point: luck is going to play an outsized role in your career, for good or for ill.

Some are anointed.

Nevertheless, support from a publisher can be a tailwind. We don't live in the world of Emily Dickinson, where someone will discover your collected works and publish them posthumously to great success. James Salter may eventually have his moment as a recognized master of late 20th century fiction, but only because a record of his books are out there.

I started Haywire Books because I had books in a drawer that I believed in, and because I knew other authors did too. My theory is that the press could be a bridge, if nothing else, a place for midlist novelists who needed a publisher to keep them going while they built their audiences and awaited prime time success. Or not. If I end up being a quasi-permanent home to a small cadre of writers, that works too. There's a gap in the market, and I'm here to fill it as best as I can.

I'll talk about some of the nuts and bolts of the industry at the end of this book, but for me the big leap was putting out my own book on my own list. The 21st century has seen the rise of a thriving self-publishing community, but the community faces very real barriers in the traditional system. Some of those barriers are related to volume; just as dark matter dwarfs the matter we can see in the universe, so self-published works dwarf the traditional book trade. Booksellers and reviewers screen out self-published books by necessity. But there's also an element of snobbery, the sense that self-published books can't be good, because if they were good they would have found a traditional publisher.

I don't exempt myself from this snobbery. I've read a handful of self-published books, mostly by people I know, but they're not the first thing I reach for. In 2018, I struggled with making that leap, because giving up a traditional career felt like defeat, a leap you don't come back from. It also felt like vanity. Why was *my* book so important that it needed to be published in 2019? Maybe I really was deluded, and this venture was nothing more than an ego project for me to foist my words, my stories, into a marketplace that didn't want them. Although I still haven't come to terms with this decision, I'm in it. *The Edge of America* is on the market, and so are the next three novels in the Haywire Books catalog: a 20th anniversary reissue of Patricia Henley's *Hummingbird House*, Mark Powell's *Firebird*, and Heather Bell Adams's *The Good Luck Stone*.

I could point to analogous ventures for comfort. In 1917, Virginia Woolf and her husband, Leonard, founded Hogarth Press. They put out a range of books from their literary community, the Bloomsbury group, but they also put out Virginia Woolf's own novels *Jacob's Room*, *Orlando*, and *The Waves*. I've read that Woolf's fiction evolved once she created her own publishing channel, that she felt free to write what she pleased without having to please a publisher. The 1920s were a time of great change in literary taste and form, comparable to the 21st century, so I like the idea of comparing Haywire to Hogarth, with the acknowledgment that I certainly am no Virginia Woolf.

More recently, Dave Eggers founded McSweeney's and self-published his debut novel, *You Shall Know Our Velocity*, as well as the first hardcover editions of *What Is the What* and *A Hologram for the King*. In 2002, when he launched the endeavor, Eggers had more standing in the national literary community than I do, having been a bestseller with his memoir *A Heartbreaking Work of Staggering Genius*, but his own story of publishing himself has not received as much commentary as one might think. The same goes for Kelly Link, another writer with plenty of literary standing, who founded Small Beer Press. In addition to publishing scores of other authors, she used the press to reissue her first book of stories, and then published the first edition of her second collection, *Magic for Beginners*. Link has a co-publisher, but the parallel is there. Small Beer Press has a niche overlooked by traditional publishers; call it "literary fantasy," perhaps, the genre Link herself is the queen of. Her press is a channel that fills a void.

I don't know Eggers and Link, and don't know why they founded their presses, or how they feel about having their own work on McSweeney's and Small Beer Press, respectively, but I suspect they had similar motivations—a gap in the market, and an opportunity to do something cool. Although they are both established literary figures, they both seem to operate a little on the edge, in a sandbox rather than a swim lane.

I can't honestly say what I'm doing with Haywire Books, or what my rock-bottom motivations are (to do something cool, or to satisfy vanity), but I will say it's empowering to create your own channel, and to have the autonomy to do whatever you want, to be in charge of everything from the book's title to its cover design (two areas authors seldom have control over). I hope it strikes a chord with readers and provides a good home for other authors. Wherever the press goes, however, I'm calling this book *So You Want to Be a Novelist.* Every novelist has a unique career, bound by her own talent, hard work, and luck, and if you want to embark on this profession, this is where you might find yourself, in a dead end with the traditional route and throwing a Hail Mary.

I'll finish where I began: if you want to be a novelist, maybe don't do it. Just about any other profession is more lucrative, and can be just as satisfying. When you're twenty years old, you don't know anything, and by the time you figure that out, you will already be on a path with no return. I would take a long, hard look at law school, or try to get an internship with an ad agency. You could be the voice for a brand on social media! If, after reading the first half of this book, you still think you want to be a novelist, part two offers some thoughts on craft—what the work itself looks like—and then part three closes with some thoughts on the book business and where you might go from here. Onward.

THE CRAFT

What Craft Is

One common cardinal rule of becoming a novelist is that you have to read a lot and write a lot. While this may be sound advice in theory, it's not particularly helpful if offered in a vacuum. Imagine sticking a would-be pianist in a room with a piano and a stack of records and saying, "If you want to be successful, listen to a lot of music and practice for 10,000 hours." Great, but what if the pianist doesn't understand the concepts of pitch, or know the scales, or understand how to build and develop motifs? Or even how best to sit at the piano? Where is she supposed to start?

Pitch, scales, motifs: these are all elements of craft, and knowing a little bit about them can help deepen your understanding of a piece of music. I imagine there's a feedback effect for musicians: you learn something about craft—say, the structure of Beethoven's four-note motif in his Symphony No. 5, the *dah-dah-dah-daahhhh* of fate knocking at the door—and then you start hearing all the variations and inversions of that motif and see how it adds an inherent structure to the symphony. Maybe that gets you thinking about the relationship between structure and motifs in general, and you start listening to other works for similar patterns. A simple observation—the naming of a pattern—might change how you listen to music and open up new layers of meaning. I imagine musicians would take this new understanding back to their own work, write a motif and then play around with it to see what's possible. Learning the craft deepens your understanding and provides focus to your practice.

The opposite may also be true. I have been listening to rock music all my life, but I know very little about the craft of drumming. I suspect I've never picked up on some important, fundamental patterns, which prevent me from ever being able to truly "hear" a rock song. All I hear in the background is *Bop! Bop! Bop! Bash!* I know the drums are there, but other than the occasional crash of a cymbal or tittering on a snare drum, I'm lost. Keith Moon was reportedly one of the great drummers of all time, yet when I listen to The Who, although I hear a lot of energy, nothing about the drumming jumps out compared to any other rock group. Maybe there are some different patterns to the drumming? Or more noise? *Bash! Bop-bash! Bop-bop buh-BASH!* I'm sure anyone who knows about drumming would shudder to hear my description of the art form, but I've always been an indiscriminate listener of rock music, so I therefore have never listened beneath the surface to understand the patterns at work.

The same holds true for novelists. You can read indiscriminately all your life, but if you never focus on the underlying structures of fiction, you're going to be lost when it comes time to write your own book. You don't necessarily have to speak the lingo of "psychic distance" or "free indirect discourse," but naming these things for what they are will help you recognize the pattern at work. It can bring some focus to your reading, and give you something to practice while you're piling up the thousand (or million) pages of your apprenticeship.

I have to admit up front that I'm a little wary of the words *craft* and *technique*. In an essay called "Writing Short Stories," collected in *Mystery and Manners*, Flannery O'Connor disparages books on the craft of writing, saying,

> I feel that discussing story-writing in terms of plot, character, and theme is like trying to describe the expression on a face by saying where the eyes, nose, and mouth

are. I've heard students say, "I'm very good with plot, but I can't do a thing with character," or, "I have this theme but I don't have a plot for it," and I once I heard one say, "I've got the story but I don't have any technique."

Technique is the word they all trot out. I talked to a writers' club once, and during the question time, one good soul said, "Will you give me the technique for the frame-within-a-frame short story?" I had to admit I was so ignorant I didn't even know what that was, but she assured me there was such a thing because she had entered a contest to write one and the prize was fifty dollars.

I'm certainly not going to argue against O'Connor that the elements of fiction work together as a unified whole, and that discussions of craft or technique won't salvage anything at the holistic level. The unfortunate truth for a budding novelist is that you can't teach such a unified vision. I think ideas for stories are like gifts, and your job is to recognize a good idea for what it is and do something with it.

That said, fiction isn't this thing that just happens, as if the novelist is some kind of savant who simply channels a vision. Craft—or technique—does exist and can be learned, I believe, with the caveat that good technique can't make up for a story lacking vision, or heart, or soul, or what Gertrude Stein called "there there."

In another essay, "Total Effect and the Eighth Grade," O'Connor argues, "I would like to put forward the proposition, repugnant to most English teachers, that fiction, if it is going to be taught in the high schools, should be taught as a subject with a history. The total effect of a novel depends not only on its innate impact, but upon the experience, literary and other-wise, with which it is approached." She was taking issue with teachers assigning books they thought would "hold the attention and interest of the students," which she believed was problematic because the novel is a form with a history, and good novelists are (or were at one time, and perhaps should be) aware of that history. O'Connor doesn't draw the connection, but it's akin to

T.S. Eliot's "Tradition and the Individual Talent." The individual talent must be steeped in the tradition to be able to make it new. To fully appreciate a good novel as a reader, O'Connor felt, you need a grounding in literary history.

Her comments may sound a little fusty today—do you really need to understand Fielding, Austen, Dickens, Eliot, James, Woolf, and Joyce to appreciate Zadie Smith?—but I suspect part of the reason is that most novelists today are working on the assumption that their readers are not steeped in the history of the novel. Zadie Smith is an excellent example, because several of her novels read as though they are playing with their literary forebears: *White Teeth* as her take on Dickens, *On Beauty* as her take on Forster, *NW* as her take on Woolf and Joyce. You can read and enjoy any of Smith's novels on their own, but just as a budding musician might do well to study the motif patterns in Beethoven's Fifth, a young novelist may find it helpful to read and compare *On Beauty* to *Howard's End*, and to consider what Smith is doing and why.

Linguists talk about *prescriptive* versus *descriptive* grammar. An oversimplified comparison of the two approaches is as follows: Prescriptive grammar says, "This is the rule. Follow it." Descriptive grammar says, "This is the pattern, and here's why it might exist." I think most linguists today are descriptivists who recognize grammatical rules are constructs, often with classist associations. The same principle holds true for the craft of fiction. *Craft*, for me, is a description of how fiction works, and how certain techniques give rise to certain effects. Are there firm rules for what you can and cannot do? Nope. Are novelists always conscious of employing a certain technique to a certain effect? Nope. Some novelists may not even be able to articulate why they made a certain decision at a certain moment. But I do believe all accomplished novelists think differently about fiction than an average, untrained reader. I have a musician friend who once observed that all Chevy car horns beep a certain note. I recently asked him about that, and he said he thought it was a B flat, but said they also beep an A note to create dissonance. Other auto brands have F or F sharp horns, he added. My friend can't go through the day without "hearing" differently from the average person. The same holds true for novelists when they approach a book—you "hear" it differently.

What follows in this section is not a traditional craft book, in which I'll lay out all the elements of technique one by one. Plenty of those books have been written, and if you feel like you need one, you could do worse than picking up Forster's *Aspects of the Novel* or Janet Burroway's textbook *Writing Fiction*. Rather, this section is an exploration of *some* of the techniques and *some* of the processes at work in writing a novel, with the goal of giving you something to focus on so that your reading and writing are not as haphazard as my approach to drumming. *Bop! Bop! Bash!* This section is about helping you "read" differently, to give you something to focus on in your practice. In the next chapter, I'll walk through one process for drafting a novel, to show what goes through my own head as I'm building out a story. As you'll see, it mostly involves asking questions and examining possibilities. It is by no means the only way to write a novel, but what I want to show is the process of invention. How does a novel get built? How do you make up characters and scenes. What happens next? Invention is the job of the novelist.

Then, I'll spend the rest of part two analyzing novels to see how they're built, beginning with a discussion of close reading and moving through various elements of craft: setting scenes, managing perspective, building the structure. This survey won't be comprehensive, but should provide some ideas for what the job is when you sit down to do the work—starting with the first draft.

How to Draft a Novel

Many if not most novelists start with an image: a character, a setting, a landscape, a situation. The source for this first image is as mysterious as the origin of the voice inside your head. It's like asking, how does consciousness emerge? Maybe it's something you see, maybe it's something you experience, maybe it's something you dream up. Whatever the reason, it's a gift, and the image grabs hold of you and says there's a story here. A person on a run, or a dead body on a beach, or an argument between a couple. Maybe it's a teenage girl showing up at a no-name gas station in rural Georgia after midnight. Sodium lights, a lone tractor-trailer across the parking lot, the clang of the door as she enters the convenience store. What is she doing there? Where is she coming from? Where is she going? Is someone after her?

This instigating image—the *abiding image*—might be a mystery, but once you set this scene, there is an astonishing array of decisions to make, whether you realize it or not. I'm not sure I would recommend thinking too much about these decisions, but if you're stuck, thinking about your choices may help you brainstorm what happens next. What happens next, of course, depends on what kind of novel you're writing. The word *genre* is a little fraught, with its connotations of commerce and class, so I prefer to think about *form*. What form of novel are you writing?

For example, here's an image that struck me recently. I was visiting my friends Ben and Laura in Oswego, New York. They are roughly my age—early middle age—and Laura was recovering from a recent hip injury. We went for a short hike at one of the nearby parks. This was in the fall, at the tail end of peak leaf season. A harvest of colors were in the trees above us, and we took our time walking through the woods.

The trail came to an end on the shore of Lake Ontario, a short drop-off to a narrow pebble beach and then a wide expanse of lake. I grew up in the South, amid man-made TVR lakes that are puddles by comparison. It startled me to see waves crashing on the beach while the three of us stood on a precipice and listened to the waves. Several trees along the edge of the drop-off had fallen, root balls still on the cliff and trunks splayed across the beach.

The day was bleak, the sky low and gray, and although it wasn't raining you could almost feel a mist in the air. The pops of yellow and orange in the woods were stark against the gray sky and the gray air and the dark gray pebbles of the beach and the bleak water. It was a beautiful setting for the setup of a crime novel, and I had an image of Laura out here walking along, rehabbing her hip, stepping up to the precipice and discovering a dead body face-down on the beach.

Before moving into the decision of what to do with this image, a few comments about the image itself. First, I recognize a dead body on a beach might be a hackneyed image. A woman alone in the woods on a misty coast stumbling on a dead body: that's not the most original opening, but so what? If it sparks your imagination, that's as good a reason as any to follow the story along. What sparked my imagination about this particular image is the landscape of upstate New York, and the endless expanse of Lake

Ontario beyond the horizon. And the wintry day, the contrast of colors: I grew up with Carolina blue skies. By the time my skies turn gray for winter, all the leaves are gone.

And then there's the question of why Laura, rather than Ben, who is out walking and discovers the body. In real life, Laura is a professor and a naturalist, and I get the sense she spends time alone at this particular park. Ben, by contrast, works corporate hours. The only time he could get out there during daylight in the late fall would be a weekend, and if it were a weekend, I imagine Laura would join him. So, the real-world Laura might be able to stumble on a dead body while walking by herself one afternoon, whereas Ben would not. Sometimes images come from real people, with real details, but that's okay. You'll fictionalize them at some point.

Finally, I think what struck me most was Laura's hip injury. She was walking a little slower, and imagining what it would feel like to hike with a grind in my hip transported me outside my own head and into the head of Laura-the-character. I know from my own experience that somewhere in your late twenties or early thirties, you start to grow conscious of your body as a finite thing—weaker, less reliable than you thought. You don't spring back like you used to. On the way to forty, then, an injured hip is no longer something to shake off and ignore. Each step would be a reminder of the gap between mind and body, mortality and the soul. And, voilà. Suddenly, we have metaphysical consciousness inside the image of the character. Laura-my-friend has become a fiction, a character experiencing something that I as the author imposed on her, something not-me and not-Laura. Something—someone—else.

Discovering a dead body while subconsciously aware of one's mortality seems like a fine place to start a novel.

But where you go from here depends on what kind of book you want to write, which may depend on what kind of reader you are. I don't read much fantasy or sci-fi or horror, so I know for me the dead body doesn't have anything to do with aliens, or government experiments gone wrong, or ghosts. With me, it's probably going to be some kind of crime novel, but it doesn't have to be—and even "crime novel" is too non-specific. If I'm writing a cozy mystery, the discovery of the body is enough. Laura sees a man face-down, maybe muffles a scream, and the scene ends. If the book is a gristly crime novel, you might have to describe more. A spatter of blood or entrails, maybe, or an animal feasting on the flesh. Or a hatchet sticking out of the back of his head. Or, the man is naked, with gruesome lash marks on his back. To ratchet up the tension even more, perhaps a child is sitting quietly on one of those tree trunks nearby. How much to describe, how gruesome or complex to make the murder, when to end the scene: these are choices, and the form of the novel will drive both the decision and the next scene.

What happens next?

In a standard crime novel or mystery, a dead body on the scene in chapter one means someone has to come out to investigate, and the person you choose as your investigator also points toward form. A small-town sheriff would turn the novel into a "country noir" in the vein of Daniel Woodrell. The small-town dynamics, and the grim underbelly of rural America, would take center stage.

You could also have a team of top-notch investigators—state troopers or a CSI crew, perhaps—and the book might become a police procedural, with a focus on the gadgetry and the analysis. Depending on who the victim is, maybe the FBI or an intelligence agency comes out to investigate, putting you in Lee Child or John Le Carre territory. It might be interesting if someone other than a cop could be the investigator: a pathologist, perhaps, or a young and inexperienced district attorney with something to prove. Possibly a social worker to take care of the child, who of course isn't speaking. Is the kid related to the victim? A witness?

You could also make this an amateur sleuth novel, and make Laura the investigator. Perhaps she's a reporter. Or maybe she knows the victim—a student of hers at the university, say, or a neighbor. Why does this case drive her into investigating? What's going on in her personal life that would inspire her to get wrapped up in a murder investigation?

If Gillian Flynn is more your speed, maybe Laura did it, and we'll get a big reveal about her mid-way through the novel. (In crime fiction, there's a decent chance that the person who finds the body is also the killer.) Or, the killer could be an ex-boyfriend, and Laura is a suspect who has to solve the crime to exonerate herself.

The dead body could also be a red herring. Nothing says this has to be a crime novel, so Laura could call the police, give her statement, and then go home to tell Ben about it.

To my mind, the macro-structure of a novel is that something is wrong in the beginning (a question needs to be answered, or a mystery needs to be solved), and the problem or question or mystery is answered in the end. In the beginning of this story about Laura, what is wrong in her life? How might discovering a dead body be a catalyst?

Here, I should note I'm entering a fiction. As far as I know, my real-life friends are not living novelistic lives, by which I mean they aren't experiencing the kind of crisis that could drive a novel. But plenty of couples do, and the secret heart of a marriage is an excellent subject.

So many decision to impose on the characters: what kind of crisis are they having, or about to have? When Laura gets home, consider manufacturing an argument. The wife tells the husband about the dead body, and he's insufficiently interested, perhaps. Why? Maybe he's thinking about some money he lost in a bad investment recently. Or, maybe he's daydreaming about another woman that he works with. Or, maybe he's just hungover. Whatever the case, the husband's not listening triggers something in the wife, and maybe she remembers something, or maybe the argument is part of a larger pattern, and for whatever reason *this* particular argument changes things.

Or, instead of an argument, maybe the wife finds it a relief to have something to discuss, to think about something other than whatever problem they're having. If not their marriage, perhaps something happening with their family. Parents going through a late-life divorce, or a sibling in rehab, or maybe a long-lost cousin from California is coming to visit. A stranger comes to town: there's a common plot. The husband and wife drive down to Syracuse to pick up the cousin at the airport, and they forget about the dead body until this evening, when they are casting about for something to say to this stranger in their home.

Another possibility: the novel could investigate suburban ennui, so maybe Ben and Laura are hosting a party. Oswego doesn't strike me as the best venue for a cocktail party of corporate go-getters, but we could shift the setting somewhere, into the Finger Lakes perhaps. If we kept it in Oswego, it might not be out of the question to have some working-class construction guys or NRA types getting together. Are they forming a little militia to protect against the long arm of the government? You could also have a group of academics, if you wanted to write a small-town campus satire.

A quick Google search of business in the region shows Xerox, Bausch + Lomb, and Paychex are all headquartered somewhere in the region. That's a far cry from *Mad Men*, but we could make Ben an executive in an optics corporation. He could be a chemist who has recently completed an MBA and risen into some type of senior management position. Working for a vision company, but he's blind to whatever crisis is emerging in their lives.

So, a cocktail party, a bull session of Bausch + Lomb executives. What are they talking about? The trade war maybe? The supply chain from China is unstable, putting their jobs at risk. Or maybe there's already a corporate restructuring underway, and a few colleagues are plotting their eminent exit. To do what? Start their own shop? Maybe instead of a cocktail party, we leave Laura and follow Ben to work at the office. What's the company culture like? How does Ben fit in? What's his team look like? What kind of work crisis could be on the horizon for him?

My real-life friend Ben has said, of fiction, "You got to dance with the one who brung you." Whatever type of character you want to write about, and whatever type of novel you want to write—these conditions will determine what you do with your abiding image. If you get stuck, start asking questions. Think about the form you're writing in, and what kind of things happen in novels like the one you want to write. Then start writing scenes.

Okay, now you have your opening image, and you've figured out generally what kind of form you're working in. You've sent Laura home to talk to Ben, or pick up the cousin at the airport, or bring the guests over for a party. Or, you've left Laura and brought in an investigator who comes to the lake, kneels pensively over the dead body, and starts thinking about who-dunnit.

What happens next?

A novel tends to start *in media res*, in the middle of things, but the general form allows you to capture entire lives over 300 pages, so consider throwing in some back story. There's an old adage that character is desire, so you might write a sentence like this: "What Laura wanted most in the world was…" Make it something small and tactile. Rather than "health and happiness," maybe something like, "What Laura wanted most in the world was a break. First her father got sick last year, and then the dog died, and then Ben needed a tooth implant, and then the car broke, and now she was in physical therapy for her hip. She couldn't remember the last time things were going smoothly—perhaps when she was twenty-five and…"

Then fill in some details about the past that might somehow be relevant for the present. It doesn't matter if the back story seems pointless. If nothing else, you're getting to know the character, and when you revise you may end up cutting Laura out of the novel altogether. The job today is to get something on the page, and to start building a world. "Sheer length persuades," Jane Smiley once said of the novel. So, make it long.

As a counterpoint to desire, fear is also a way drum up information about a character. "More than anything else, Ben was afraid of driving behind logging trucks, because he worried a log would come loose and impale him on the freeway." Suddenly, you have a scene with Ben: get him on the freeway behind a logging truck. Maybe a log is a little wobbly. Maybe a log actually comes off and he has to swerve around it. Maybe he hits it and ends up dead in a ditch, or wakes up with some kind of neurological disorder.

Or maybe he swerves and gets to work, at Bausch + Lomb, and he starts telling his coworkers about it. Sam and Vicky and Jennifer. Plus, the intern Ben can never remember the name of.

When you get stuck again, maybe jump over to someone else. Vicky has been standing there listening to Ben's story. What does Vicky do at the company? What's her story? What does she want? What's she afraid of? Does she know Laura? Did she know the dead guy on the beach? Is her brother a cop who came out to investigate?

So many possibilities! This is how a novel unfurls, for me at least. I zigzag around from character to character, scene to scene, writing what interests me and what feels right for what I want to write today, and after a few months of this, I'll end up with 300 pages. You can't write 300 pages without some semblance of a story showing up—a few central characters, a situation.

When you get stuck, you can always reread the beginning and think, "Oh right, there was a dead body on the beach." Go back to Laura and Ben, or to the small-town sheriff investigator. At some point, you'll figure out what crisis you're writing about—a murder mystery, or a marriage falling apart, or a corporate accounting scandal—and you can make up an ending.

I don't know how to tell you to end it, except to say you answer the question you asked in the beginning, and in a way appropriate for the form.

If it's a cozy mystery, gather all the suspects in a room, or out by the lake, and have the investigator unmask the criminal. For a grisly crime novel, have the killer corner Laura. She has to grind through her injured hip to escape. Maybe along the way she's gotten a gun from one of her NRA friends and shoots the killer, or a tree could fall on him during a dark and stormy night out at the original scene of the crime. Who knows? At this point, who cares? You're the one writing it, and you're the only one who will know if it's a goofy ending or not. If the victim was a Russian gangster, the FBI team may need to raid some kind of criminal safe house. Or if the story is about the social worker and the child, the ending might be the social worker visiting the child one last time, after the crime is solved, and having tea with the grandparent guardians.

If it's not a crime novel, but rather about the couple's marriage falling apart, or not, end it with one of them sitting in a car in the driveway, in the dark, and staring at the yellow lights of the house against the blinds (echoing the yellow leaves against the gray sky from the abiding image), thinking about whether to go up and knock on the door. Trying to find the courage to say the un-sayable, which might salvage the marriage.

Novels are about pattern-making, and along the way you will likely stumble on these visual echoes. Yellow leaves against dark skies, yellow light in a window at night. When those echoes emerge, it's a sign that you're doing something right. Keep going. E.L. Doctorow once said that writing a novel is akin to driving on a highway at night. You can see only as far ahead as your headlights will send you.

This chapter is about getting a draft on paper, 300 pages or so, a cast of characters, the arc of a story. Revision, and then publication, and then building a career as a novelist all present different problems, but it starts with getting the first draft on paper, which is about recognizing an image of worth, and then building scene after scene, making decision after decision, until you have something that resembles a novel.

Reading Like a Novelist

Fiction writing is the art of *invention* and then *translation*. Fiction first is about inventing characters, settings, stories. Making stuff up, which I think might be a largely subconscious and therefore mysterious process. A strong sense of curiosity and openness can ready you for the task, and continuously asking questions might guide you from one page to the next. The act of writing is about translating these things in your brain into words on a page. Making sense of the voice in your head, which is a conscious and therefore intentional process. You learn how to do these two things—make stuff up and translate it into words on the page—by doing it. Sitting your butt in the chair and filling page after page with words.

Craft is not about invention or translation, but about shaping what you have so that it can be as good and as clear and as compelling as you can make it. Think of craft as a toolbox, the equivalent to fiction what pitch, scale, and timbre are to music. Terms such as *point of view* and *plot* are primarily descriptors to help us understand how a novel is put together. I think the best way to learn craft is by studying other works, investigating how they are put together and learning the techniques other authors employ. Studying craft can offer you a way into a book, the way a mechanic might look under the hood of a car to study its engine. Consider a Rothko painting for comparison. Most of his paintings were on big canvasses with a couple of stacked wide stripes. They're the kind of painting someone might look at and say, "Well, that's easy. I can do that!" Or, "What am I supposed to get out of this?"

When you have that kind of reaction while looking at a piece of visual art, it can be helpful to take a time out, remind yourself that you don't know everything, and then look critically for a few minutes. Interrogate the piece: What am I seeing? What's happening? In the case of a Rothko painting, you might see a big reddish orange canvas with a dark blue—navy, maybe?—square on the upper half. The edges of the square kind of blur into the red-orange. You look a little closer and see a lighter orange square beneath it, filling the bottom half of the painting. But the colors aren't pure. The borders are blurred, and the edges of the navy square are kind of muddy. And actually, now that you look at it, the blue isn't even a solid blue, it's a blend of darks and lights within the shade of navy, so that the square kind of pulses when you study it, and the colors change depending on where you focus.

Keep staring, and you start to see just how complex the painting is, and how it plays with your perception. You might find it emotionally moving for the way it pulses with life, and for the way the warmth of the orange washes over you while you focus on the navy. Or you might find the piece intellectually stimulating because it forces you to think about how your eyes focus on one object at a time, while the rest of your field of vision is a blur, and everything about your vision boils down to patterns of light and color as illustrated in the Rothko. Or you might simply delight in the interplay between the apparent simplicity and the underlying complexity, the wit behind a clever joke. Who knows? My point is that by taking a step back to focus on one element of the painting—in Rothko's case, his use of color, and how what appears to be a simple navy square on an orange background is anything but simple—leads you toward analysis. You go from the particular to the universal, the concrete to the abstract. You start with colors and shapes, and that leads you to ideas about perception.

*

This move—from the particular to the universal, and from the concrete to the abstract—is fundamental to understanding how fiction works. When you read fiction, to study it, one approach is to get down to the sentence level and interrogate it. Ask questions: Why did this word follow that word? Why did the author break the paragraph here? What does this line of dialogue tell us about the character? What question is the author raising here that needs to be answered? Why is this compelling? And sometimes, what even is happening here?

For example, let's look at the opening few pages of Cormac McCarthy's novel *All the Pretty Horses*. This novel is set around 1950 and is about a teenager named John Grady Cole and his adventures on horseback in Mexico. At the beginning of the novel, his father is somewhat out of the picture, his grandfather has just died, his girlfriend has dumped him, and his mother is about to sell the family farm and move off to San Antonio. McCarthy is a good case study because he has such a distinctive style. His prose is recognizable and strikingly clear when you get into it, but I think it can be a little opaque for someone approaching it for the first time. He is unusual in that he seldom tells you what his characters are thinking. He is an impressionist who shows you their actions and records their words and trusts you to figure out what is going on inside their heads. *All the Pretty Horses* opens:

> The candleflame and the image of the candleflame caught in the pierglass twisted and righted when he entered the hall and again when he shut the door. He took off his hat and came slowly forward. The floorboards creaked under his boots. In his black suit he stood in the dark glass where the lilies leaned so palely from their wasted cutglass vase. Along the cold hallway behind him hung the portraits of forebears only dimly known to him all framed in glass and dimly lit above the narrow wainscoting. He looked down at the guttered candlestub. He pressed his thumbprint in the warm wax pooled on the oak veneer. Lastly he looked at the face so caved and

drawn among the folds of funeral cloth, the yellowed moustache, the eyelids paper thin. That was not sleeping. That was not sleeping.

What do we make of this passage? I can say that for me, the first sentence is odd. When I first read it, I had to look up the definition of "pierglass" (it's a kind of mirror you hang on the wall). Unpacking what it literally says, John Grady walks into the door, and when he does, the whoosh of air causes the candle to flicker, first when he comes into the hall and again when he shuts the door. Why render it this way? Why not simply say, "When John Grady came in the door, the candle flickered"? Obviously, McCarthy's way of saying it sets a different tone. The book on the whole asks you to slow down, as a reader, to experience the laconic cowboy life, so he's indicating from the first sentence what kind of book you're in for. In this first paragraph, McCarthy also buries his lead, which is the dead grandfather lying in state. You get the image of the candle, and then the creaky floorboards, and then the cold hallways and the photos on the wall, and then you get John Grady mashing his thumb into the candle wax, and then—only then—do you see the dead man. The double phrase— "That was not sleeping. That was not sleeping"—is uncharacteristic for McCarthy, in that it takes you inside his character's mind, and we see John Grady is experiencing a kind of denial. It probably took him a moment, coming into the hallway, to register and process his dead grandfather lying in state. What McCarthy has done, when you pause to analyze the paragraph, is show you the workings of his character's mind. These sensory inputs—the candleflame, the chill air, the melted wax—come at John Grady impressionistically, and because he doesn't know how to process it all, he takes a moment to put his thumb in the candle wax before acknowledging his grandfather's body. This is grief made manifest through images.

Over the next few paragraphs, John Grady (or "he," since McCarthy hasn't told us his name) goes outside and stares at the stars for a while, "a thin gray reef beginning along the eastern rim of the world." A train whistles by, and then he goes back inside where a woman is at the stove. She greets him, "Buenos días, guapo," and then goes back to fixing breakfast. After he pours a cup of coffee, this is the first exchange of dialogue in the book:

> I appreciate you lightin the candle, he said.
> Cómo?
> La candela. La vela.
> No fui yo, she said.
> La señora?
> Claro.
> Ya se levantó?
> Antes que yo.

We learn a few things from this exchange. We know we're on a ranch somewhere in the American southwest, and John Grady's family employs a few Hispanic workers. In this dialogue, we learn something about John Grady's character. His grandfather is lying dead in the other room, yet he still says thank you to the cook. He's learned her language and is willing to converse in it (even if English is his default).

McCarthy doesn't translate the Spanish for us. I don't know why, except to suggest there is a certain amount of artifice in translating something, which he tends to shy away from. If you speak Spanish or take time to plug it into Google translate, you see that "la señora" (presumably either John Grady's mother or grandmother here, and it turns out to be his mother) was the one who lit the candle. She was up early, before the cook—awake before her son arrives home from a night out. If you translate this into modern casual English, you can infer a few more things:

> Thanks for lighting the candle.
> It wasn't me.
> Mom?
> Yep.
> She's already up?
> She got up before I did.

You can almost see him wince. We don't know what he was out doing all night, but when your parents wake up before you get home, that can be a problem. You're busted, for one thing. As long as he was home before Mom got up, they could have maintained the fiction that he was home at a respectable hour. Alas, not the case. Putting ourselves in her shoes for a moment, her father has just died, so we can imagine she's grieving. We soon learn John Grady's father is out of the picture, which means Mom is in charge of this ranch, so she's also likely got a number of responsibilities. Estate planning for her dead father, getting her head around the ranch's finances, et cetera, et cetera. No wonder she was up early. The question is, where is she now? What are she and John Grady going to do?

There's more to say about the opening to *All the Pretty Horses*, but what I'm doing here is called *close reading*, an approach to examining a text that involves digging into it word by word, line by line. Good books hold up under a close analysis, and even offer more for the attentive reader willing to dig in. This is how we'll be walking through the elements of craft over the next few chapters, and how I would encourage you to train yourself to read going forward. I have to warn you that the process of becoming a novelist, and learning to read like a novelist, may take some of the fun out of reading. Read enough books like this, and you may no longer be able to sit down and simply enjoy the story. You'll always be examining the seams of a book to see how it's constructed, just like my musician friend "hears" a B-flat when he hears the beeping of a Chevy car horn. I imagine it's the same in every field: a good graphic designer can't look at a logo without either admiring its craft or puzzling over some odd choice in the colors or typeface. A mason will notice a careless splatter of concrete in a brick wall. A photographer will notice if a picture has an odd saturation, or if the subject had less-than-optimal lighting. When you read as a novelist, you start to notice when someone's point of view gets wonky, or when a metaphor feels out of place for a particular character, or when the story gets predictable.

As a counterpoint to close reading, you'll also want to look at a novel's big-picture structure. The novel is an accommodating art form, so the parameters for what a novel is are pretty wide. After all, the form accommodates both *The Great Gatsby* (about 200 pages) and *War and Peace* (about 1500 pages) but excludes short stories (say, 1-50 pages) and novellas (say, 50-150 pages). In her *13 Ways of Looking at the Novel,* Jane Smiley defined a novel as a "long prose narrative with a protagonist." I might shorten it to "long prose narrative," because novels such as Jennifer Egan's *A Visit from the Goon Squad* and Colum McCann's *Let the Great World Spin* don't have a single central protagonist. Rather than debate what exactly counts as a novel, I'll note that whatever you're calling a novel is going to be long enough that you have to think about how it's put together. Structural elements may include:

- How long is it?
- Is it broken in to chapters or parts? How long are each?
- Is it told in the first person or third person voice?
- How many characters do we follow?
- If it has multiple characters, is there a pattern?

These are all things you can look at before you even begin a book. Once you start reading, remember my suggestion about the big-picture structure of a novel. The beginning asks a question, and the ending answers it. For a mystery, someone has been killed in the beginning, and the killer is unmasked in the end.

A company called The Great Courses puts out college lectures on DVD (and now a streaming service). One of their courses is The English Novel, taught by Dr. Timothy Spurgin. I would recommend this course to anyone interested in the history of the novel, particularly his lectures on Jane Austen. Spurgin notes that *Pride & Prejudice* is a perfectly structured novel precisely because it introduces a problem in the beginning, works out the problem, and solves it in the end. The problem, of course, is that the Bennett family has dwindling fortunes. The property is tied to Mr. Bennett and cannot pass to their five daughters, so they need to find at least one rich husband who will be able to take care of the wife and sisters after Mr. Bennett's death. The novel has one of the most well-known opening lines in all of literature: "It is a truth universally acknowledged, that a single man in possession of a good fortune, must be in want of a wife." The entire novel is baked into that sentence—the relationship between love and money, the family's desire for such a man to show up and marry one of the Bennett sisters, the provincial outlook of Mrs. Bennett in particular (the gossipy tone of the sentence, the presumptiveness of its sentiment). From the opening scene, you can map out the chapters, who is courting whom, and trace the power dynamics between Elizabeth Bennett and Mr. Darcy over a sequence of events that eventually leads to their engagement.

Scenes build out a structure: a country ball, or a tour of the neighborhood, or the arrival of a letter, a proposal, a visit to the neighbors, et cetera, et cetera. Austen may render each of these events with an amusing tone, and as a reader you may enjoy going from beat to beat, gossiping along with each of the characters, feeling your heart flutter with the arrival of a new suitor or seeing the irony of mismatched lovers, but underneath it all is a careful structure. Each scene has a *function* (e.g., "visit the Darcy estate so Elizabeth can learn he is actually very generous"), and these help bridge the problem from the beginning with the conclusion in the end. In the beginning, Elizabeth is headstrong and wants to marry for love. Mr. Darcy may be rich and handsome, but she doesn't love him at first. But a sequence of events, such as learning about his generous character, soften her and prepare her for the eventual match. The structure is A to B to C, problem to resolution.

The question of what's wrong in the beginning works well to unpack the structure of more complex books. One of my favorites is Russell Banks's *The Sweet Hereafter*, which is set in a small town in upstate New York. In the opening chapter, a school bus driver gets in a horrifying wreck and kills many of the town's children. The book is broken into five long chapters (almost novellas in themselves), each narrated by a different character: the bus driver, then one of the parents, then an ambulance-chasing lawyer who comes to town, then one of the students who survived but is paralyzed, and finally back to the bus driver. There's no mystery in the beginning: you know the bus accident happened, and you know the driver, Dolores, did it. There's also not much, on the surface, that seems capable of resolution. All these children have been killed. Where do you go from there?

From a novelistic stance, what's wrong, it turns out, is that this event happened in a small, close-knit community. Everyone relies on one another in a way unique to small towns, and this event threatens to destroy the entire community. The town's future is in doubt, literally because a generation of children have been killed but also metaphorically because no one knows how to recover from the trauma. The opening question is, will this small town find a way to heal and survive? The town itself becomes a kind of character, which justifies the shifts in perspective from one character to the next (rather than having a single, central protagonist). One major complication is when the lawyer shows up, because he's trying to drum up a class-action lawsuit that may permanently divide the town. In the end, it is one of the children (the fourth narrator, Nicole), who rejects the lawyer and makes a kind of uneasy peace with Dolores the bus driver. There's no happy ending in such a novel, but Banks at least offers the possibility of healing and reunification. That's the big-picture structure.

This approach of asking "What's wrong at the beginning of the novel?" isn't perfect. I'm not sure how one would answer the question at the beginning of *The Great Gatsby*, in which the narrator, Nick, is a young adult striking out on his own after college. He moves to a fictional version of Long Island and is trying to find his way at the beginning of his career. The novel, however, quickly becomes the story of Jay Gatsby and his years-long quest for the love of Daisy. Who is the protagonist, Nick or Gatsby? It's easy to see the pattern of the problem-and-resolution in Gatsby's story: he is trying to use his fortune to impress and woo Daisy, but he winds up shot in the end. As a witness to these events, Nick grows disillusioned, gives up on landing his career out east, and moves back to the Midwest.

You see this pattern frequently, in which a first-person narrator tells the story of another, larger-than-life character. It's the pattern of *Moby-Dick* (Ishmael narrating about Ahab), *All the King's Men* (Jack Burden narrating the rise of Willie Stark), Russell Banks's *Affliction*, and Philip Roth's *American Pastoral*. It's also the pattern in *Don Quixote* (narrated by Sancho Panza), and the Sherlock Holmes stories (narrated by Dr. Watson). In each of these novels, the larger-than-life character is unable to tell their own story (they often end up dead in the end), so someone else has to narrate their tales. In Elena Ferrante's Neapolitan novels (which opens with *My Brilliant Friend*), a narrator tells the story of her lifelong friendship with Lila, who has disappeared late in life. Lila is somewhat larger-than-life, but because she has disappeared she is not able to tell her own story. By investigating the life of Lila, however, the quartet of novels serve as a vehicle for the narrator to investigate her own life. Who is the brilliant friend, Lila or the narrator? Who are the books about?

Recognizing this pattern will change how you read books like this, because the structure provides some clue about the ending (just as you know a murder mystery will eventually be solved by the sleuth). It can also give you a clue about how to structure your own book. Say you want to write about a larger-than-life character but you don't have a good way in. Consider looking for someone nearby, who can serve as a witness and who might be moved by the story of your central figure. Let that side character be the narrator, and see where that takes you. The structure automatically gives you an opening: you need to lay out the occasion for when the narrator first meets the larger-than-life character (i.e., Ishmael goes aboard the Pequod, Nick moves to Long Island, Jack gets an assignment as an aide to Willie Stark). From that instigating event, your job will be to follow the story, possibly by asking one question after another until you reach a conclusion.

When I approach a book for close study, I have two things in the back of my head. The first is Henry James's word *donné*. He said that as a critic, you should grant every book its *donné*, or its given. What he meant by this was that every author who sets out to write a book has certain parameters in mind, and it's only fair to weigh a book against those parameters. If I'm going to critique, say, a Berenstain Bears book, I should critique it as a book written for children. You can only expect so much human insight, interesting language, and plot development in a thirty-page illustrated book written for small children. James would have you ask, "What is this book trying to do? And how is it succeeding?"

Not every novelist is aspiring to be the Great American Novelist, and there's no sense grumbling that a book doesn't do what an author never set out to do. James Salter's *Light Years* is a slow, plodding, literary novel. I think it's an excellent book, but it's not trying to be a page-turner, and you can't weigh it against, say, *Gone Girl*. Likewise, Michael Connelly set out to write police procedurals with the Harry Bosch books. They're great mysteries and a lot of fun to read, but because of what his purpose is, it would be unfair to fault him for focusing so much on the mystery of a case and less on Harry's psychological baggage. What is this book trying to do? And how is it succeeding? Those questions take you beyond the gut-reaction "I don't like this" or "I love this" and into an analytical frame of mind, which is the way you read as an aspiring novelist studying the craft.

The second thing I think about when I think about close reading is something my high school art teacher, Mike Biggs, said about analyzing art. I don't know if he made this up or stole it from someone, but he had a method of art criticism he called FOGATE, an acronym for:

- Focus
- Open your mind
- Gut reaction
- Analyze
- Translate
- Evaluate

Applying this method to reading fiction, *Focus* means you've shut off your phone and set aside a block of time to dedicate to the book. *Open your mind* means a willingness to step outside yourself. "I've heard McCarthy has a weird style, but I'll give it a shot." *Gut reaction* is permission to give an immediate sense of the book. "That first sentence was weird. What's that about?" *Analyze* is where you try to lay out what exactly is happening. Look up the Spanish words if you don't know them; reread the dialogue to make sure you know who is speaking. *Translate* means you start asking questions. "What does this mean? Why did the author do it this way?" Finally, *Evaluate* is where you answer the question of whether the author succeeds in doing what they set out to do.

What each of these critical methods—James's *donné* and Mr. Biggs's FOGATE—have in common is they ask you to move beyond a gut reaction, to step outside yourself and approach a novel with a sense of humility, a sense that you have something to learn. In part one, I wrote about my professor Bret Lott's ethos of *I know nothing*. If you can internalize it, this sensibility keeps you open and curious, which I think is the right way to approach any course of study. To return to the Rothko painting, your gut reaction might be that it's just a couple of stripes of paint on a big canvas, but once you pause, focus on the work, open your mind, and start investigating what you see, the painting opens itself up to you. When you start reading novels more closely, with the mind of a novelist, you'll be surprised what might open up to you.

SETTING THE SCENE

The basic building block of a novel is *scene*, which is a sequence of actions occurring in real time, the same as you would have in a play or a movie. The lights come up, and the actors are in a particular setting. They talk and interact and do stuff, and then at the end of the scene the lights go dim and the set is rearranged. Or, in the case of movies and television, the camera cuts to a new time and place. In fiction, scenes consist of two elements: *description* and *dialogue*. Dialogue of course means people talking to each other—he said, she said. Description can be external description (painting the picture of what you see) or internal (describing what a character is thinking).

Together, description and dialogue bring a scene to life, and they create a kind of movie in the reader's mind. In his book *On Becoming a Novelist*, John Gardner calls this the "vivid and continuous dream," and it is one central tenet for how fiction works. Nearly every novel is built around a sequence of scenes that add up to a story. You might be able to point to an exception, some experimental novel that resists the idea of scene altogether, but scene is almost fundamentally linked to narrative: a person experiencing an event in time. One good exercise for a beginning novelist, then, would be to study how other authors develop scenes. How much detail does an author provide? What is the balance of description to dialogue? What is the balance of internal thoughts versus external rendering? How long are the scenes? How many scenes does the novel have? Are scenes broken up by chapters? Space breaks? Or do the scenes run together?

The length of a scene can be particularly instructive. My sense is that many beginning novelists—or short story writers trying their hand at their first novel—write very short scenes of a page or a few pages. Sometimes all you need is a couple of pages to spit out the scene, but I would recommend you practice writing longer scenes—five, ten, twenty pages. A twenty-page scene can be difficult to write because it forces you to dig in to really unpack something interesting. You might feel like you're writing filler, and that may be true at first. But when you stick with a scene and keep trying to tease out good material, you'll eventually have a richer story than one that skims the surface of a lot of scenes. Reading plays can be helpful for learning how to unpack a scene. Most plays have a few scenes, but it would be inefficient for a playwright to have too many because you don't want your live audience getting bored with all the scene-shifting. Consider: Cormac McCarthy's play *The Sunset Limited* is ninety minutes of two guys sitting in a room having a conversation. That could be an interesting conceit for a novel as well: two people having a conversation. Sandor Marai's short novel *Embers* is just that: two old friends meet and have an overnight conversation. Marai gives us plenty of back story and flashback scenes to fill out his narrative, but the novel is essentially one long conversation. The same is true for Mario Vargas Llosa's much longer *Conversation in the Cathedral.* Two friends catch up by chance one day and go to a bar, and then they discuss the protagonist's father and the history of the country.

I'll talk more about handling time in a couple of chapters, but for now my key point is that a scene is the single most basic element of fiction, and a good novelist will stick with a scene to develop it rather than hit a couple of high spots and then move on.

*

If a scene is comprised of description and dialogue, how much should you describe? A general guideline is that you want to provide enough detail to show the reader what you aim for them to see, without bogging them down in unnecessary information. One key phrase to keep in mind is "significant detail." For example, Chekhov suggested that if you have a gun on the mantel in Act One, it should go off by Act Three. You don't want to sit around describing all kinds of things that ultimately don't matter, because the story will lose focus. However, there's no straightforward formula for how much to describe, because every novelist is different. Every book is different. How much detail you give will depend on what kind of story it is and what kind of writer you are.

On one end, you have someone like David Foster Wallace, a maximalist who piles detail upon detail to flesh out his scenes. Here is the opening of *Infinite Jest*:

> I am seated in an office, surrounded by heads and bodies. My posture is consciously congruent to the shape of my hard chair. This is a cold room in University Administration, wood-walled, Remington-hung, double-windowed against the November heat, insulated from Administrative sounds by the reception area outside, at which Uncle Charles, Mr. deLint and I were lately received.
>
> I am here.
>
> Three faces have resolved into place above summerweight sportcoats and half-Windsors across a polished pine conference table shiny with the spidered light of an Arizona noon. These are three Deans—of Admissions, Academic Affairs, Athletic Affairs. I do not know which face belongs to whom.

Even if you're not familiar with the novel, you can tell from this passage that it is satiric in tone. The pompousness of academia is rendered with pompous prose, and by describing the scene with such detail, you sense the narrator is making fun of it—and thus invites us to join him in bemusement. We, the readers, are in on the joke. Is it too much? Possibly, but the reader who will want to stick with *Infinite Jest* for 800 pages will enjoy rollicking in the excess of details—the "consciously congruent" posture and the "spidered light of an Arizona noon." I'm not sure how you could finish a Wallace novel without enjoying the witty turns of phrase sentence by sentence. In this respect, the way the author renders a scene is a signal to readers about what kind of experience they are about to have.

On the other end of the spectrum might be the spare, declarative prose of Kent Haruf, whose novel *Benediction* opens:

> When the test came back the nurse called them into the examination room and when the doctor entered the room he just looked at them and asked them to sit down. They could tell by the look on his face where matters stood.
>
> Go on ahead, Dad Lewis said, say it.
>
> I'm afraid I don't have very good news for you, the doctor said.
>
> When they went back downstairs to the parking lot it was late in the afternoon.
>
> You drive, Dad said. I don't want to.

Here, you don't get any whimsical details about the light entering the room or the doctor's half-Windsor knotted tie. Haruf doesn't spell out anything about Dad Lewis's diagnosis, but you know it isn't good. Wallace's prose serves to characterize the narrator—a highly intelligent slacker who might be rolling his eyes at the situation and who might also be on the Asperger's spectrum—whereas Haruf leans on dialogue to characterize Dad Lewis, a stoic and reserved old man facing the end.

The story, the characters, and the situation drive the appropriate amount of details, but all of this—story, character, situation, style—derives from an author's personality and vision. The world according to David Foster Wallace is much different from the world according to Kent Haruf. It's well worth an aspiring novelist's time to study how different authors render scenes, and how much detail they provide, but you will have your own vision and your own natural style, and I believe practice is the only thing that will help you find your voice, which will then help you find the right balance for how much to describe.

Similar principles hold true for dialogue. Some authors have pages and pages of witty dialogue, whereas others rely on a few choice lines to convey what they need the reader to see. The balance will vary by author, but there's a good chance a beginning writer is either putting in too much dialogue or too little.

On one hand, dialogue is more like a *translation* than a *transcription*. If you sat around transcribing conversations, you'd find people waste a lot of breath on filler: "Hi." "Hi." "How are you today?" "Just fine. How are you?" In a list of ten rules for good writing, Elmore Leonard recommends leaving out the boring parts. A lot of real-world dialogue is boring, so if you're filling page after page of empty filler conversation, you might need to pare it back.

On the other hand, if you're a short story writer trying your hand at your first novel, your instinct might be to skim along the surface and offer a few lines of dialogue here and there without actually digging into the conversation. Novels give you (some) room to breathe, so it's okay to have some back and forth, or to have a character speak for more than one sentence before the other character responds.

Let's make up a scene here to think about how description and dialogue work together. Say, two characters are on a walk through the woods. Call them Katie and Brian, and they're in a county park in upstate New York, on a trail that will lead them to the roaring shore of Lake Ontario. It's a bleak day in late fall, low gray clouds, a bite of mist in the air. Tall trees surround them, sycamores and white oaks, maybe, with bright yellow leaves stark against the gray autumn air. What are they going to talk about?

Well, one thing that keeps popping up in my life is the issue of aging parents and grandparents, something I discuss frequently with my wife, so I might make up a scene like this:

"I talked to my mom this morning," Katie said.

"Oh yeah? How was her trip?" Katie's mother had just gotten back from visiting her parents in Central Florida.

"It was okay. My grandfather's not doing very well."

"Worse than before?"

"You know my mom. I couldn't get a clear story out of her, but it sounds like they really need to move him into an assisted living community, because my grandmother can't manage it all." She winced as she stepped over a log in the trail, and Brian stopped to make sure she was okay. "He's getting up in the middle of the night," she continued, "turning on all the lights, and he'll start cooking eggs or something at two a.m. My grandmother apparently has to get up every night to coax him back into bed, and my mom's worried he might be getting violent."

Brian whistled. His own grandparents were long gone, and he was already thinking about his aging parents down in Virginia.

"I don't know. In one breath, she's telling me she might need to fly back in a week or two to see how things are going, but then she's telling me about her bunions."

I'm not holding this up as some kind of brilliant scene, but there are a few things to point out. First, I didn't write "Katie said," "Brian said" with every line of dialogue, because I think it's clear who is talking. A paragraph break usually indicates that the next speaker is coming in, so you can safely assume Brian is the one who asks, "Worse than before?" A tag every few lines can be helpful, but it would be repetitive to tag every single line "he said," "she said."

Second, I have three types of description in this passage. The first is *explanatory description* ("Katie's mother had just gotten back from visiting her parents in Central Florida"). When you are rendering a scene in real time, external references come up. Sometimes it's clear from context what is going on, but sometimes a line of explanation can be helpful.

The second type of description I have is *scenic description* ("She winced as she stepped over a log in the trail, and Brian stopped to see if she was okay"). This is what you might see if you were watching a movie or play. In fiction, the reader isn't watching a screen, so you may have to describe what you want them to see. I wanted the reader to see that particular image for a few reasons. As I laid out in the chapter on drafting a novel, a character's injured hip could be a significant detail, so here I introduced an injury to give you some texture of Katie's life, and also to foreshadow something that could be significant later in the story. I also had Brian pause to wait for her to help characterize him as a decent guy. You know that even as they are talking, his mind is on her injury (and thus her general wellbeing). Finally, I wanted to show a pause in Katie's monologue. What she's saying is difficult for her, so a person in real life might be speaking in fits and starts, trying to gather her thoughts. Rather than say explicitly, "She paused to gather her thoughts," I gave a description of them walking, stepping over a log. Description within a scene of dialogue can help modulate the pace of what is being said.

A third type of description in the scene is *internal description* ("His own grandparents were long gone, and he was already thinking about his aging parents"). We are in Brian's point of view, and his interest in Katie's grandfather is partly empathetic (caring about what she cares about) and partly selfish (he has his own family problem to deal with). So, Brian might be a decent guy—pausing to wait for her while crossing the log—but he's also caught up in his own issues. Perhaps that might indicate some friction between them. Is he really listening to his wife? Or maybe his own experience helps him better connect to his mate. Perhaps the root of empathy is experience. Whatever the case, unlike movies or the theater, fiction takes us directly inside the minds of the characters, which you can do within a scene.

One final comment about the above scene. I used the words "said" to attribute the dialogue rather than "exclaimed" or "mumbled" or "moaned." One general rule of thumb most craft books and writing teachers will tell you is that "said" is the best way to attribute dialogue. The reason is because "said" is a neutral, functional, almost invisible word, like "the" or "was." The reader will register it but will also skip right along to the next word, whereas other ways of attributing dialogue might call attention to the prose. Imagine rewriting the scene:

> "I talked to my mom this morning," Katie mumbled.
> "Oh yeah? How was her trip?" Brian boomed.
> "It was okay," Katie said with a sigh. "My grandfather's not doing very well."
> "Worse than before?" questioned Brian.
> "You know my mom," Katie replied.

The adage *show, don't tell* means the narrator should be invisible, whereas this rewrite would be *telling*—the narrator tells you Katie is mumbling and Brian is booming. As an invisible word the reader can ignore, "said" shows, allowing the reader to maintain what John Gardner calls the "vivid and continuous dream." Telling with words like "mumbled" and "boomed" might give readers pause, because they will subconsciously register the narrator's heavy-handed explanation.

Only a dogmatist would tell you that you always have to show rather than tell, and that you always need to say "said" rather than something else. As with the spectrum ranging from Wallace's maximalism to Haruf's minimalism in description, you're free to render your scenes the best way you see fit. Telling can be okay. It can add a little personality to the narrative, which might work in certain modes. Light or humorous novels can get away with "Katie mumbled" and "Brian boomed," whereas a spare or hardboiled narrative would need to rely on "said." You're free to choose which words you use, but keep in mind the words should be appropriate for the kind of narrative and the kind of style you are employing.

One recommendation I have is that you avoid dialogue attribution tags that conflate speaking with gestures: "Katie laughed," "Brian shrugged," and the like. Plenty of authors might write a sentence like this: *"This is so much fun,"* Katie laughed. What they mean is: *"This is so much fun,"* Katie said with a laugh. The difference between "laughed" and "said with a laugh" might be pedantic, but you don't literally laugh words. You speak and you laugh; you can do both at the same time, but they are two different actions, yet plenty of authors conflate the two actions. I suspect authors use gesture-words such as "laugh" out of convenience. It's faster to say "laughed" rather than "said with a laugh," and authors assume readers will understand what they're trying to say. What the word "laugh" conveys to me, however, is that you are either lazy or muddled—lazy if you don't want to write out exactly what you mean, or muddled if you actually don't know what you are saying and believe a person can somehow laugh out a sentence.

I wouldn't blame you if you are now thinking, *Ok boomer.* After all, the distinction between "laughed" and "said with a laugh" really is nitpicking. My caution for you is that such nitpicky readers are out there, and you are signaling something to them, intentionally or not, with the words you select. You want to make sure you fully understand what you are communicating.

In a YouTube video, the author Sharon McCrumb discusses the pronunciation of "Appalachia" ("Appa-LATCH-ya" versus "Appa-LAY-sha"). She cites the town of Derry or Londonderry in Northern Ireland, and says that if you go into a convenience store to ask for directions to the town, the clerk will tell you how to get there regardless of what name you call it. Calling it Derry suggests you are an Irish nationalist (or sympathize with them), whereas calling it Londonderry suggests you sympathize with the British unionists. Your word choice tells the clerk who you are, where you are from, where your sympathies lie, and whether they can trust you.

Communication is laden with pitfalls, and the word "laughed" in dialogue attribution is one of them. Give your readers a sign that you are not thinking sharply, and they might decide they can't trust anything in your prose. One slip, and you could undercut everything.

*

One syntactic pattern running rampant through scenes in American fiction, particularly literary fiction, is the independent clause + comma + present participle (-ing word). A paragraph in a typical literary novel might read something like this:

> She went down to the beach, hauling a towel and suntan lotion and an assortment of other items necessary for proper relaxation. She unfolded her towel on a flat strip of sand, listening to the rhythmic crashing of waves. She walked to the water's edge, squishing her toes through the wet sand and letting the cool water wash over her feet. She inhaled the salt air, enjoying this beautiful day.

This paragraph is obviously an exaggeration, but you get the idea. Independent clause, comma, present participle phrase. If this paragraph appeared in a workshop, a reader would no doubt circle the "She" – "She" – "She" – "She" and maybe jot a note about not starting every sentence the same way. A workshop reader may also circle all those participle phrases and say, "Mix up your syntax."

Why are writers drawn to this particular syntax? And more importantly, what's wrong with it?

The intended effect of this sentence structure seems to be a kind of impressionism. It's a turn from narrative action to lyric description, which we expect in literary fiction. Time stops when you shift from past tense ("She unfolded her towel") to the ongoing, present participle ("listening to the rhythmic crashing of waves"). It seems instinctive for authors, when they want to write something beautiful, to reach for the nearest present participle and offer a few token lines about the setting—even better if the natural world can be described. Water, trees, the moon, the wind. Literary fiction is supposed to be about reflection rather than action, after all. Literary fiction that stops time with a present participle is an easy way to slow down and "show" a scene.

The literary critic James Wood cites Flaubert as responsible for a type of stylized prose driven by visual details. Flaubert is arguably the godfather of the modern realist novel, yet Wood argues in *The Broken Estate*, "The failings of contemporary writers reveal certain weaknesses in Flaubert's greatness." Flaubert may be responsible for our mantra of *show, don't tell.* Paint a scene and let the meaning simmer below the surface. Yet this method, for Wood, only works in the hand of a master like Flaubert. In lesser hands, Wood writes, "Contemporary writing ... takes Flaubert's controlled visual sweep, shaves off some of its richness, and merely cinematizes it."

Wood's general theory of fiction, which he lays out in *How Fiction Works*, is that creating rich characters creates life on the page, which is the function of narrative art. His objection to post-Flaubert painterly prose is that it skims the surface of life. It keeps the character at arm's length. Again from *The Broken Estate,* he writes:

> Yet the danger of Flaubert's heavily visual details is that they flatter the visual over the unseen, the external over the interior (and Flaubert is not really a great novelist of interiority), that writing becomes primarily, and in some cases only, a way of making us feel "almost *materially* the objects [it] describes."

My complaint about the failed lyric syntax (independent clause, comma, present participle) is that while the author is striving for beautiful lyricism, the result too often is a dreary stasis. Time stops for no apparent reason other than to linger over external details. You could make the case for subtext (bobbing in a warm sea could evoke the protection of the womb, perhaps), but this metaphorical resonance has to be earned through precise observation and rigorous prose. The syntactical structure I'm arguing against is perfunctory, not rigorous—lazy, rather than lyric. It shows, but it shows imprecisely.

This syntax isn't always bad, and I'm a little more forgiving of it with dialogue: *"Blah blah blah," she said, setting her coffee mug on the table.* Sometimes, you just need to have two things happen at once, and the present participle is a way to accomplish that. But, given the prevalence of this syntax in American fiction, I would suggest those moments of static, repetitive prose are good doorways for revision. If you find yourself sliding into several sentences in a row that make use of present participles, one solution is simply to rewrite them. Try a longer cumulative sentence or two, interspersed with shorter declarative sentences. For instance, the beach example I started with could be rewritten:

> She hauled her towel and suntan lotion and other accouterments down to the beach, where she set herself up on a flat strip of sand not far from the water's edge. The waves crashed rhythmically. The beach was deserted. After unfolding her blanket and stowing her belongings, she walked toward the water and squished her toes through the wet sand, inhaling the salt air as the waves washed cool water over her feet and up to her shins.

This revision is better than the original, I suppose, because at least there's some syntactical variety, but it doesn't really solve the philosophical problem of meaning. What's the point of describing this woman by the beach? Why should we care about her? What is she thinking? Therein lies Wood's objection. She doesn't have any spark of life, any sense of interiority.

One diagnosis of the problem with the comma -ing syntax is a lack of confidence on the part of the writer. It often reads as if an author has stopped time to figure the scene out for himself. But when the author doesn't believe, the reader won't believe either. If you don't know what the scene looks like or what the character is going to do next, the result might be a static reflection and indecisive syntax. Rewriting the comma -ing syntax might be all you need to do, but you might want to consider why you employed the syntax to begin with. Don DeLillo once said, "Writing is a concentrated form of thinking." If your prose is imprecise, perhaps your thinking is imprecise. Why were you aiming for quiet lyricism? Why did you stay on the surface rather than diving into the character? *Could* you dive deeper into the character?

*

Before leaving the discussion of scenes, I'd like to walk through the first chapter of Ann Patchett's novel *Commonwealth*, which tells the story of a fractured family over fifty years. It opens in the 1960s, at a christening party at the home of Fix and Beverly Keating. Fix is an LAPD detective, and a district attorney he barely knows, Bert Cousins, crashes the party with a bottle of gin. Beverly leaves Fix for Bert, and the novel follows their families and their children into the present day. The novel as a whole would make an interesting study in structure, but the first chapter in particular is a case study in setting a scene.

Earlier I suggested that a long scene can be interesting. I find dinners and parties difficult to write, but they are among the most satisfying scenes to read, when done well, because there is so much opportunity for characters to cause a scene. Think about how much drama happens at family get-togethers! The first thirty pages of *Commonwealth* are one extended sequence at the christening party, and we see the catalyst that ends Fix and Beverly's marriage right in the first paragraph:

> The christening party took a turn when Albert Cousins arrived with gin. Fix was smiling when he opened the door and he kept smiling as he struggled to make the connection: it was Albert Cousins from the district attorney's office standing on the cement slab of his front porch. He'd opened the door twenty times in the last half hour—to neighbors and friends and people from church and Beverly's sister and all his brothers and their parents and practically an entire precinct worth of cops—but Cousins was the only surprise.

Here, we get a dramatic moment in the first sentence: a character who knocks things off-kilter. Gin sounds a little out of place, dangerous even, at a christening party, and right away we know Albert Cousins is going to make something happen in Fix's life. In the second sentence, we learn Fix knows Albert but only vaguely, and can't understand why the man is here. The third sentence tells us a great deal about the Keatings' life—that Fix is likely a cop, that they are long-standing and popular members of the community, that their family lives close enough to come to a party. And because the Keatings are solid members of a solid upstanding community, you know Cousins and his bottle of gin are *really* dangerous.

The next page gives us some dialogue that further fleshes out the characters and the situation:

> "Fix," Albert Cousins said. The tall deputy DA in the suit and tie put out his hand.
>
> "Al," Fix said. (Did people call him Al?) "Glad you made it." He gave his hand two hard pumps and let it go.
>
> "I'm cutting it close," Cousins said, looking at the crowd inside as if there might not be room for him. The party was clearly past its midpoint—most of the small, triangular sandwiches were gone, half the cookies. The tablecloth beneath the punchbowl was pink and damp.
>
> Fix stepped aside to let him in. "You're here now," he said.

One way to read this chapter is by studying the power dynamics between Fix and Cousins. Fix doesn't even know Cousins goes by Bert, so he knows Cousins wasn't invited. He knows Cousins is crashing, yet he does the polite thing, shakes the man's hand and invites him in. Fix is the conservative, ruffle-no-feathers, upstanding community member, and Cousins is the disruptor, the man who brings gin. Cousins knows he's not been invited, and because Fix calls him Al, Cousins certainly knows Fix knows Cousins is arriving uninvited. Yet the two men talk as though Cousins is not crashing the party. If this is a power negotiation, Cousins has the upper hand.

After a little more surface-friendly dialogue, Fix ushers him into the house and closes the front door. We then get our first glimpse of Beverly. After Fix closes the door, he thinks:

> Beverly had told him to leave it open so they could get some air, which went to show how much she knew about man's inhumanity to man. It didn't matter how

many people were in the house. You didn't leave the goddamn door open.

Beverly leaned out of the kitchen. There were easily thirty people standing between them—the entire Meloy clan, all the DeMatteos, a handful of altar boys plowing through what was left of the cookies—but there was no missing Beverly. That yellow dress.

Inside the Keating home, we learn a little more about them: they are Catholic, and the party really is a pretty good size. We see Fix has his own opinions about his wife and her stance on what's proper. Again, he is the old conservative. You'll never see him wearing shorts and a T-shirt and telling people to "take it easy."

Then there's the yellow dress. We know a good bit about these characters—Irish and Italian Catholics, middle class cops. You can sense the house is a point of pride, though it's likely small by 21st century standards. Patchett hasn't described the lawn at this point, but you know Fix is the kind of guy who mows it every Saturday and fertilizes it on schedule. The yellow dress stands out because at this point, it's the most distinctive visual detail we have of these characters. Cousins is a "tall deputy DA in a suit and tie." In another page, Patchett will describe Beverly's best friend as "too thin and too tan and when she straightened up she was wearing too much lipstick." But Beverly's yellow dress is the star of the show. You get the sense she is a woman who turns heads. We don't even know what kind of dress it is; the sheer fact of it being yellow, in an otherwise nondescript world, makes it distinctive and therefore significant.

If you didn't already sense that the marriage is under stress, and that Cousins's appearance is going to turn things, Cousins gives Beverly a nod down the hall, and "By reflex Fix stood straighter, but he let the moment pass." We soon learn Fix is a detective, which means he is well attuned to subtext, gestures, mood. He's picking up on the wavelengths in the room. Two pages later, he brings the bag of gin to the kitchen, and Beverly asks him what it is. "Fix held up the gin, and his wife, surprised, delivered the first smile she'd given him all day, maybe all week."

Less than five pages have passed, and all that has happened is Cousins shows up unexpectedly, and Fix lets him in and brings the gin to the kitchen. Yet we know so much about the Keatings lives, and the underlying tension in their marriage, and we know Albert Cousins is not going to be good for the family dynamic. He's not going to go home at the end of the party and allow everything to go back to normal.

The women send Fix out to the store for ice, and when he arrives home, everything has changed:

> Fix hadn't checked his watch when they'd left for the market but he was a good judge of time. Most cops were. They'd been gone twenty minutes, twenty-five tops. It wasn't long enough for everything to change, but when they came back the front door was standing open and there was no one left in the yard.

The front door turns out to be a significant detail. Not only does it help characterize Fix and Beverly's relationship, but it also signals the change. Fix and his brother go inside the house and find everyone sweating in the kitchen, making drinks. Beverly is slicing oranges (a sensual fruit), and Cousins and another DA are standing there with their jackets and ties removed, shirtsleeves rolled up, juicing oranges for the mixed drinks. You wouldn't catch Fix Keating in his shirtsleeves juicing oranges with the goddamn front door wide open, that's for sure. Again, if this is a power negotiation between Fix and Cousins, Cousins has the upper hand. He's made himself the star of the party and earned the affections of Beverly, whereas frumpy old Fix had to go buy ice like the responsible family man he is.

The party continues, and Patchett continues to build the world and the tension. When the kitchen clears out, Fix takes up his turn making drinks. He and Cousins are the only ones in there, and Cousins offers to relieve Fix. Fix then brings up a case where they had worked together, acknowledging out loud that he'd been trying to remember how he knew Cousins. Still, neither of them brings up the fact that Cousins has crashed this party, and Fix doesn't kick him out. Instead, he sends Cousins to go find the baby.

Cousins wanders around the house—snoops—and eventually finds the baby with Beverly, getting a diaper change in a bedroom. They have an intimate moment, in which he thinks about his own wife and how he was supposed to be home hours ago, and then he kisses Beverly: "There was an almost imperceptible shift between them." Then she tells him she's drunk and he should go bring the baby to Fix. "And don't tell him anything else, mister," she says.

Of course, everything has changed. Fix and Beverly had a rift between them, and the surprise appearance of Albert Cousins is all it took to bring that rift to the fore. We get all of this through scene: descriptions of a yellow dress, a bottle of gin, the front door. What characters say to each other, and what they refuse to say aloud. A drilling down into one afternoon, one moment in the lives of these characters.

Establishing Perspective

If the "vivid and continuous dream" of fiction is akin to building a movie in the reader's mind, then *scene* is about what happens on screen from moment to moment. What you see and what the characters say to each other. *Perspective* is about who the camera is focusing on (*point of view*) and how close the camera is zoomed in (*psychic distance*). Perspective is closely linked with two other elements of craft: *voice* (what the prose sounds like thanks to the diction and syntax) and *character* (the people we're developing).

To start with some definitions, point of view refers to the grammar of how the characters are presented. You probably remember from grade school that in English, we have:

- First person singular – "I did this"
- First person plural – "We did this"
- Second person – "You did this"
- Third person – "He/she/they did this"

It's really a question of who is speaking and to whom. In the first person, you have an "I" narrator who is telling the story. In the rare second person story, you have a "you" that the narrator is addressing. In the third person, you have a few options for the narrator:

Third objective is somewhat uncommon, and offers a fly-on-the-wall perspective, unfiltered through any consciousness. The narrative is somewhat flat, or possibly hard-boiled. Examples in this mode include Dashiell Hammett's *The Maltese Falcon* and maybe some of Hemingway's short stories—"Hills Like White Elephants," for example.

Third close lets us into the head of one character. You could almost "translate" it directly into a first-person narrative without losing anything. The narrative voice will meld to the voice of the consciousness of the character. The final chapter of *Ulysses* ("Penelope") is in third close.

Third limited is one of the most common perspectives for American fiction. Again, the story is limited to one particular character's perspective, but there is an unnamed, unacknowledged narrative voice telling the story separate from the character. I believe Jane Austen invented this mode, and her books are excellent examples. She writes about her characters with a gentle, humorous irony, offering commentary on them that the characters would not be able to narrate themselves.

Third close and third limited both follow one character at a time. Novels in these modes may shift to other characters, but there will be a chapter break or space break to indicate you are moving to a new character.

Omniscient novels have a "voice of God" perspective—an external narrator (like third limited) but one that can float into anyone's mind or across time anywhere in the narrative. Omniscient used to be common (think Tolstoy), but is a little unusual in 21ˢᵗ century American fiction.

Closely related to point of view, *psychic distance* refers to how close we are to the character's mind. Consider the zoomed out omniscient voice at the beginning of Gabriel Garcia Marquez's *One Hundred Years of Solitude*:

Many years later, as he faced the firing squad, Colonel Aureliano Buendía was to remember that distant afternoon when his father took him to discover ice. At that time, Macondo was a village of twenty adobe houses, built on the bank of a river of clear water that ran along a bed of polished stones, which were white and enormous, like prehistoric eggs. The world was so recent that many things lacked names, and in order to indicate them it was necessary to point.

This passage has long, all-knowing sentences, it jumps around in time, and it refers to the character by his full name—a stately presentation of the scene. Meanwhile, here is the opening of Zadie Smith's *NW*, which is so zoomed in on the character that she doesn't even give you a glimpse of them, just fragments of thought and impressions:

> The fat sun stalls by the phone masts. Anti-climb paint turns sulphurous on school gates and lampposts. In Willesden people go barefoot, the streets turn European, there is a mania for eating outside. She keeps to the shade. Redheaded. On the radio: I am the sole author of the dictionary that defines me. A good line—write it out on the back of a magazine. In a hammock, in the garden of a basement flat. Fenced in, on all sides.
>
> Four gardens along, in the estate, a grim girl on the third floor screams Anglo-Saxon at nobody. Juliet balcony, projecting for miles. It ain't like that. Nah it ain't like that. Don't you start. Fag in hand. Fleshy, lobster-red.

It can be disorienting to be inside someone's head like that, claustrophobic, but part of Smith's project in *NW* is to present the variations of people in one particular section of London, and she presents the diversity through the voices of the characters, their minds at work. Garcia Marquez's project, on the other hand, is to present a myth of people in a place, as though rewriting the Bible, so he needs a wider lens. The downside is that everything in *One Hundred Years of Solitude* generally "sounds" the same. He seldom gives you a stream-of-consciousness, so for most of the novel you don't "hear" his characters' minds like you do when you zoom in like Smith.

The first-person voice also has the equivalent of psychic distance, in terms of how immediate the narrative is, how close to the narrator we are. Toni Morrison's *Jazz* has one of the most intriguing openings I've ever read:

> Sth, I know that woman. She used to live with a flock of birds on Lenox Avenue. Know her husband, too. He fell for an eighteen-year-old girl with one of those deep-down, spooky loves that made him so sad and happy he shot her just to keep the feeling going.

That word, "Sth," sounds like someone sucking her teeth, which brings you right up close to her. She hasn't told you anything yet, but you already feel intimacy with her. The clause "I know that woman" reinforces that we're being treated to some gossip. Morrison hasn't set us anywhere in particular, but you feel like you're leaning across a table to hear the narrator as she tells you about someone who is standing across the room. You're psychically close.

Other first-person novels employ what's called a retrospective narrator—a narrator looking back—and the perspective in these novels is often less intimate, as the narrator is removed in time from the action. For example, this passage from Tana French's *Faithful Place*, in which a middle-aged detective must reckon with a crime that occurred twenty years ago:

> My father once told me that the most important thing every man should know is what he would die for. *If you don't know that*, he said, *what are you worth? Nothing. You're not a man at all.* I was thirteen and he was three quarters of the way into a bottle of Gordon's finest, but hey, good talk. As far as I recall, he was willing to die a) for Ireland, b) for his mother, who had been dead for ten years, and c) to get that bitch Maggie Thatcher.

You can probably hear the difference between the Morrison and French passages. The French passage has a colloquial tone—"but hey, good talk"—but it sounds less like a narrator leaning in to tell you something and more like someone leaning back to ruminate.

For me, the default perspective is a novel written in the third person, past tense voice, in limited omniscience. What I mean by default is that this particular perspective is so common (at least in contemporary American fiction) that it is easy to understand and allows the author to remain more or less invisible. Many books are written in the present tense (e.g., John Updike's Rabbit novels), but the present tense adds a noticeable voice to the story. You "hear" a little personality in the present tense. This can work wonderfully, but like using a dialogue tag other than "said," the reader will register it. When the reader registers something, you make the job a little harder on yourself because you suddenly have to maintain a consistent voice or the book will sound off-key. The past tense is a little more forgiving.

I say third limited is the default, but it's probably a coin-toss between that and the first person. In some ways, the first person voice is the most natural way of telling a story ("I was flying to Syracuse the other day, and let me tell you what happened at the airport"). When humans are sitting around the campfire, or in a bar, they tell stories from their own first-person perspectives. But for me, the first person voice also raises questions about who the narrator is and whether they are reliable. When you encounter someone in real life and they start telling you a story, you know who they are and make a judgment about how trustworthy their story is, based on what you know about them. With a novel, a first-person narrator is starting with a blank slate, and you only have the language itself to help you evaluate the narrator. More on the first-person in a bit.

For now, let's look at the third-person perspective. I personally like a fully omniscient novel, but as with a novel written in the present tense, an omniscient narrative is a delicate thing. You have to establish and then maintain a kind of grand voice so the reader trusts they are in capable hands. I remember sitting in a workshop in graduate school, and some poor soul had turned in an omniscient story. We spent about an hour discussing the point of view and whether it was "okay" to move into multiple characters' minds. We were asking the wrong question for that hour. Of course it's okay, but the story was off-key in a couple of ways none of us in the class could articulate. In hindsight, I think what was missing was (a) an establishing sentence to let us know what the story was going to do, and (b) control over psychic distance. Just like a movie might be jerky if you start zoomed out and then you have a quick-cut to be zoomed up close, an omniscient narrative that opens wide might need a little breathing room to zoom in. One good example is Min Jin Lee's novel *Pachinko*, an omniscient story that covers several generations of a Korean family in exile in Japan. The book opens:

> History has failed us, but no matter.
> At the turn of the century, an aging fisherman and his wife decided to take in lodgers for extra money. Both were born and raised in the fishing village of Yeongdo—a five-mile-wide islet beside the port city of Busan. In their long marriage, the wife gave birth to three sons, but only Hoonie, the eldest and the weakest one, survived. Hoonie was born with a cleft palate and a twisted foot; he was, however, endowed with hefty shoulders, a squat build, and a golden complexion. Even as a young man, he retained the mild, thoughtful temperament he'd had as a child. When Hoonie covered his misshapen mouth with his hands, something he did out of habit meeting strangers, he resembled his nice-looking father, both having the same large, smiling eyes. Inky eyebrows graced his broad forehead, perpetually tanned from outdoor work. Like his parents, Hoonie was not a nimble talker, and some made the mistake of thinking that because he could not speak quickly there was something wrong with him, but that was not true.

First off, who is speaking in that first sentence? Who is the "us" that history has failed? And who is this person to so blithely dismiss the failure of history? The second sentence immediately drops you into an omniscient narrative voice, a voice removed from the nameless characters and from our present time. The paragraph introduces you to Hoonie and gradually gets closer to him, describing him from the outside (the cleft palate, the large eyes), and then letting us into his psyche (he is the one who knows why he doesn't speak quickly). That zooming in over a long paragraph is the hallmark of omniscience—its challenge to write and its pleasure to read.

A limited third voice keeps the story consistently with one character, and we get a space or a chapter break to signal we're moving to another character. Once you establish that pattern, you have the freedom to go wherever you need for the story. "Limited" is short for "limited omniscience"; you may be limited with the camera focused on one character, but you are free to zoom in and out of the person's head, same as in a fully omniscient story. The difference is that the camera doesn't go quite as wide, and therefore the story feels more contained, and perhaps more accessible.

A good example of a novel in roving limited third is Jamie Attenberg's *The Middlesteins*, which bounces around among different family members during the parents' late-in-life divorce. Attenberg stays with a single character in each chapter, but within the chapter, she treats us to a humorous narrative voice that zooms in and gives us a flavor of who each character is. For instance, this section about a character Rachelle, thinking about her mother-in-law, Edie:

> Rachelle's mother-in-law was not well. Rachelle wouldn't have described her as sickly, though, because there was nothing frail about her. Edie was six feet tall, and shaped like a massive egg under a rotating array of silky, shimmering housedresses that seemed to make her glow. But Edie had had stent surgery six months before on her rotting thigh—a side effect of diabetes—with another surgery scheduled in a few weeks, and also lately

Rachelle had noticed that two of Edie's teeth had gone black. Concern stabbed her directly in the heart. Also, she was disgusted. Yet she could not bring herself to mention it.

It wasn't her job, anyway, to talk to her mother-in-law about dental care.

You can hear Rachelle sitting around grumbling about her mother-in-law. This could be translated into the first person without missing much, so you might categorize it as close third rather than limited third person. The difference between those two perspectives doesn't really matter all that much, to me, but what does matter is the way Attenberg assigns a "voice" to the prose. The term for this is *free indirect discourse*, in which the third-person perspective slides into the character's voice. You can hear the character as sure as if she were talking out loud to you. The word "anyway" in that last line, set apart by commas, makes the sentence sound colloquial and gives it life. Think how dull it would be if Attenberg had kept the voice neutral and written, "It wasn't her job to talk to her mother-in-law about dental care." That revision would be *fine*, but it wouldn't be worth quoting in a book on craft.

Voice can come in word by word, or it can come in by syntax. The word "anyway" brings Rachelle's passage above to life. Here is another passage from *The Middlesteins*, from Rachelle's father-in-law, Richard Middlestein, enjoying his newfound freedom as a divorced man shopping in Ikea:

And what a bargain that place was! Sure, it was a lot of crap he didn't need, and his father, who had owned a high-end furniture shop in Jackson Heights for decades, would probably roll over, coughing, grumbling, cursing in his grave if he saw what Richard's new bed frame was made of. But he was not a rich man—by some standards, maybe, to starving children in India, he probably lived like a king—since the market had wiped out half their retirement fund, so he had no choice in the matter.

You can point to a few individual words in this passage that create voice—for instance, the word "sure" at the start of the second sentence, or the word "maybe" in the dashed-off section—but it's the syntax at large, the parenthetical asides, the lists, the cumulative nature of the sentences, that give this passage its sound.

Earlier, I mentioned the first-person voice raises a few issues in terms of who is narrating. The Tana French and Toni Morrison passages I quoted are both trustworthy, straightforward narrators. If you are writing a first-person novel and intend for the narrator to be trustworthy, one of your jobs in the opening pages is to establish a rapport with the reader, the same as if you were meeting someone for the first time. Many first-person novels open with an introductory greeting:

- "Call me Ishmael." (*Moby-Dick*)
- "My name is Ruth." (Marilynne Robinson's *Housekeeping*)
- "My name is Frank Bascombe." (Richard Ford's *The Sportswriter*)

Other novels open with a narrator acknowledging a weakness, or a limit to what they know. Tana French's first novel, *In the Woods*, opens with a short evocative prologue and then introduces the narrator with: "What I warn you to remember is that I am a detective. Our relationship with the truth is fundamental but cracked, refracting confusingly like fragmented glass." Here, your narrator is telling you he holds the truth in high regard, but acknowledges his perspective will be flawed. That serves to build trust while simultaneously preparing you for any unreliability to come.

The unreliable narrator is nothing new. The 18th century British writers who essentially invented the novel as we know it played around with the fallibility of narrative. Henry Fielding's *Tom Jones*, for instance, gives us a standard novel of manners (in the style of Samuel Richardson), but every other chapter is a kind of meta-fictive commentary on the story—the narrator undercutting his own story by calling attention to the fiction.

Nevertheless, it's astonishing how easily the average reader is lulled into a narrative, only to be caught off guard if they find out there is more going on than there seems on the surface. Take Gillian Flynn's *Gone Girl* as an example. (If you haven't read the book, I'm about to ruin the twist, so skip this paragraph and the next if you don't want it spoiled.) The story opens with alternating chapters: a husband whose wife has gone missing, and the wife's diary entries. Although he contends his innocence, the husband is a prime suspect, and the diary entries seem to point the finger at him as a murderer. About halfway through the novel, the real wife's voice comes in, and we learn she has been trying to frame him for her murder. She wrote the diary entries to point police (and the reader) toward the husband. Those entries are the classic unreliable narrator.

They also read falsely, to me anyway. When I first read the book, I thought the story was just badly written:

> Tra and la! I am smiling a big adopted-orphan smile as I write this. I am embarrassed at how happy I am, like some Technicolor comic of a teenage girl talking on the phone with my hair in a ponytail, the bubble above my head saying: I met a boy!
>
> But I did. This is a technical, empirical truth. I met a boy, a great, gorgeous dude, a funny, cool-ass guy. Let me set the scene, because it deserves setting for posterity (no, please, I'm not that far gone, posterity! feh). But still. It's not New Year's, but still very much the new year. It's winter: early dark, freezing cold.

You get pages and pages and pages of this cheery, grating voice. I suppose people's diary entries might be so banal, but I kept asking why Flynn was wasting so much space in this novel on such obnoxious prose. Then the twist happened, and you see the wife has much more going for her than her faux diary would indicate. I didn't see the twist coming, but I also wasn't shocked by it. Maybe I'm a grumpy pessimist, but the cheery voice of the diary didn't sound quite honest to me. I was looking for the grit underneath, which we get when Flynn pulls back the curtain on the wife's true character. The evidence was right in front of us, in the wife's badly written journal entries, yet readers are generally so credulous that *Gone Girl* became the novel of the decade, at least until *Where the Crawdads Came Along* and pulled something similar.

Irony, in fiction, is when the narrative (but not necessarily the narrator) clues you in on something the character isn't aware of. If you have a murder mystery written in third person, you can have the intrepid investigator in one chapter and the murderer in the next chapter. You may know whodunnit, but the fun comes from watching the investigator go down wrong turns, and maybe put themselves into danger. Think about the horror movie when you know the killer is lying in wait for a character, but the camera remains fixed on the character so you can't see the shadow lurking in the hallway. You know something bad is about to befall this hapless character, but the character remains blithely innocent. That's irony.

With the first-person voice, irony takes on new complexity, because irony exists when the reader knows something the narrator doesn't. An old Hollywood mogul reportedly once said, "Irony is what goes over the heads of the audience." With a first-person point of view, the challenge comes when the credulous reader fails to pick up on the irony; it goes over your head, so that you misread the book. A classic example is Mark Twain's *Huckleberry Finn*. Is Huck a racist narrator? Yes. Does that book throw around the N-word? Yes. Does it show us life in the Antebellum south, and a black man playing to the racist stereotypes of blackface? Yes. To the credulous reader, *Huckleberry Finn* is a racist book that has been justifiably banned from classrooms for generations…but that's only because the main point of that book has gone over the heads of so many readers.

The novel is narrated by Tom Sawyer's pal, Huck Finn, a backcountry boy in search of adventure. He runs away from home and his drunkard father and sets sail down the Mississippi River, where he encounters Jim, a slave he knows who has run away. Jim joins Huck for further adventures, and here is where the charges of racism begin. While Huck and Jim sail down the river, Jim seems to be exhibiting all the racist stereotypes white Americans have imposed on black Americans for generations: the happy slave performing a minstrel show in a country dialect, whose sole function, on the surface, is to entertain this white boy on his adventure. If that's all that was going on, this novel would be a scourge on American literature.

What scholars will point out, however, is that if you read Huck as a classic unreliable narrator, if you step outside his perspective and into Jim's perspective, you suddenly see what Mark Twain is up to. As a slave, Jim has run away for fear of being sold down the river by his current master. If he is recaptured in slave territory, he knows he likely would face unspeakable consequences. Although Huck is a boy and thinks of Jim as his friend, Huck has all the power in this relationship. If Jim does anything to upset Huck or spoil the adventure, all Huck has to do is yell out for help and Jim would be captured, beaten, and returned to his owner if not lynched on the spot. Jim's life is not his own so long as they are in Missouri, Kentucky, Mississippi. Therefore, what does he do? He puts on a happy minstrel show as a survival mechanism.

This is subtle irony, because the careful reader (or the reader with a good teacher) can point to passages where we see Jim making a calculus that Huck is unaware of. For instance, when Huck first comes across Jim, he is excited to confess what he's been up to, that he ran away from home: "Well, I warn't long making him understand I warn't dead. I was ever so glad to see Jim. I warn't lonesome now. I told him I warn't afraid of *him* telling the people where I was. I talked along, but he only set there and looked at me; never said nothing." What is Jim thinking in this passage? Huck is so wrapped up in his own story that he doesn't stop to wonder what Jim is pondering (or even that Jim might have his own private, deep thoughts), though when we stop to ask the question, Jim is likely weighing his options as an escaped slave. Is Huck about to turn him in? Can he trust Huck?

On the next page, Huck finally asks how Jim got to be where he is:

> He looked pretty uneasy, and didn't say nothing for a minute. Then he says:
> "Maybe I better not tell."
> "Why, Jim?"
> "Well, dey's reasons. But you wouldn't tell on me ef I 'uz to tell you, would you, Huck?"
> "Blamed if I would, Jim."
> "Well, I b'lieve you, Huck. I—I run *off*."
> "Jim!"
> "But mind, you said you wouldn't tell—you know you said you wouldn't tell, Huck."

From Huck's perspective, this passage is pretty innocuous, because he doesn't fully understand the meaning of what Jim has done, doesn't understand that if Jim is caught, he might be brutally beaten or even murdered. But what we see from Jim's perspective is a kind of calculation. He's looking for a way out of the state, and Huck might be his ticket. At the very least, he doesn't want Huck going around talking about Jim as a runaway slave to anyone. So, he appeals to Huck's sense of fairness—don't tell on me, and I won't tell on you. It's a gambit that psychologically aligns Huck to Jim, and Jim secures Huck's promise. There are passages like this throughout the novel, that show Jim as thoughtful and subtly calculating, and it all goes right over Huck's head.

I will say, here, that *Huckleberry Finn* is not my favorite novel by any means. I don't particularly enjoy reading the dialect page by page, and I'm not here to argue it needs to be on every American's high school curriculum. The repeated use of the N-word is off-putting, and I think students need a good teacher to put it in context, to discuss the institution of slavery and the history of the minstrelsy, and to perform a close reading to show what is happening beneath the surface. I bring the novel up here *because* of the controversy around it. I do think it's a powerful book that lays bare America's racial divide, and also points toward reconciliation, the genuine bond that forms between Huck and Jim. But to get to that reading of the novel, you have to wade through details that are repulsive on the surface. The novel shows what's possible in a first-person voice, as well as the price you might pay for it—namely, that so many readers have approached the novel straight, and missed the point completely.

Whatever perspective you choose, your ultimate job is to give the reader a story, which at rock-bottom is about characters involved in a sequence of events. Perspective is about character. It's about which character you put at the center of the scene, and how you develop them. There's plenty of woo-woo craft talk in books and on the internet about making your characters come off the page, everything from creating little dossiers about what your character ate for breakfast to sitting down in every scene and mapping out what specifically the character wants to achieve.

All of that is fine advice, and I'd advise you try anything that works for you. Your job as a novelist is to be interesting, page by page, and then to build out a story: a sequence of events involving characters. Beyond that, just about everything is fair game, and may depend on what form of novel you're writing. Fantasy and some science fiction novels have characters that aren't human. What makes them interesting? Is it the human-like characteristics? Or the way non-humans throw humanity into relief, or the escape from humans altogether? I honestly don't know and can't advise in developing fantasy characters. I suspect world-building is part of the fun of fantastic fiction, which means you need more details around setting than you'd need in a standard realist novel. I recently asked a friend what the big deal was around *Game of Thrones*, and she cited all the competition for power, and the back-stabbing, and the sex and murder. In other words, human, soap-opera stuff. There's little escape from character development.

In the realm of humans in fiction, you can't traffic in the issue of character long before you eventually have to confront the issue of consciousness, which is what makes us human. I believe it was

Norman Mailer who suggested a novelist needs a friend in every profession, someone you can turn to for information as you build out your stories. I think that's sound advice, not only so you have a good resource in any profession, but so that you can expand your understanding of humanity. We live in an age of bubbles. We choose a political stance, a candidate, a suite of stores and restaurants that speak to our Brand as a human being. I think it's probably healthy for everyone, but especially novelists, to seek out people outside your bubble. Look for the oddballs and try to figure out what makes them tick. At the same time, try to cultivate what Keats called "negative capability." Keats said this in praise of Shakespeare, arguing that what made Shakespeare great was his ability to get rid of his self and truly embody his characters. Is Shakespeare Hamlet? Lear? Falstaff? The fool in *Twelfth Night*? He's everywhere and nowhere. It's akin to empathy, what I'm talking about, the ability to understand what it's like inside the mind of another human being, a capacity I think is unique to fiction among the arts.

Neuroscientists hell-bent on understanding the brain and reducing human activity to electrical impulses or bits of data are still, in 2020, wrestling with the metaphysical issue of consciousness, what some philosophers have termed the "hard problem of consciousness." How exactly does our brain experience the world? How are we self-aware? Why do we have memories? Where the hell does the voice in our head come from? Novelists take that voice and put it on the page. The word "anyway" from the Attenberg passage a few pages ago: "It wasn't her job, anyway, to talk to her mother-in-law about dental care." To develop your characters, I would recommend doing whatever you need to do to land on the "voice."

In opera, composers will assign what's called a *leitmotif* to a character, a recurrent theme that we come to associate with a character. If you go on YouTube and do a search for "Wagner leitmotif," you can pull up several examples, such as "Siegfried" in *Die Walkure*. This leitmotif goes something like "dum dum… dum dum…du-du-dum!" It helps characterize the figure and also serves as something of a reminder to help anchor us when the figure is on screen. The word "leitmotif" is applied a few ways in the world of fiction, but it generally refers to a repeating pattern or idea, a helpful concept when it comes to developing characters.

A leitmotif could be a particular pattern of speech or collo-quial catch-phrase, or it could be a concept rooted in a charac-ter's psyche. In Henry James's *The Portrait of a Lady*, the central character, Isabel Archer, is a woman in want of a husband, but she also wants to live a free life. At the beginning of the novel, she has met a wealthy aunt and traveled with her from America to England, where she meets her invalid cousin Ralph. When Ralph's father grows ill, Ralph persuades him to leave a fortune to Isabel so that Isabel may be completely free. We watch as Isabel negotiates a series of suitors—a British aristocrat, an American textile magnate, and an American expatriate and widower named Gilbert Osmond. She ultimately chooses to marry the worst of the bunch, Osmond, a marriage encouraged by another member of their social circle, Madame Merle.

Osmond turns out to be a psychologically manipulative and a moocher who has married Isabel for her fortune. Although she appeared free in the beginning of the novel, and seemed to have freely chosen her spouse, we learn that Osmond and Madame Merle had conspired and manipulated Isabel into choosing him. In the second half of the novel, we witness her developing consciousness, until she finally sees clearly who Osmond is and what she has done with her life. Toward the end of the novel, she visits the dying Ralph, and then she decides to return to her husband in Italy. Why does she do it? Osmond has a daughter named Pansy, so perhaps Isabel is returning for her step-daughter's sake. Or perhaps she is going to grab her step-daughter and return with her to England. The ending is ambiguous but also confounding, because you are rooting for her to exercise her freedom, yet you also see she is trapped by conventions and obli-gations.

The idea of *mystery*—of not knowing what happens or what motivates a character—is often what makes literature capital-L Literature. The conventional marriage plot would end with a marriage and a happily ever after. That makes for a neat and satisfying story, but it's also not true to life. In *The Portrait of a Lady*, James has consciously framed the narrative to show how a marriage plot can be a *plot*, as in a scheme, as in Gilbert Osmond and Madame Merle plotted against Isabel. James brings us deep into her consciousness, and indeed the climactic moment of the book is not so much a dramatic action but a dramatic realization. Isabel spies Osmond seated in a room while Madame Merle is standing, a posture that runs against social conventions and indicates there is more to Osmond and Merle's relationship than Isabel had realized. The plot comes into focus for Isabel and for the reader, yet although James spends pages and pages showing us Isabel's thought process, she's still something of a cipher. We don't know what she is doing at the end, or why. We can speculate, but the end is ultimately a mystery.

Key point: It's okay to leave something unresolved. Sometimes those rough edges—or flaws—are what make a book interesting. An AI system may soon be able to write a perfect novel, with all the right beats in place, but such a story won't be as interesting as a human novel that shows people acting illogically, inexplicably. A novel with unresolved mystery.

The leitmotif of freedom—and whether Isabel is truly free—runs through *The Portrait of a Lady* and is at the core of her character. Another way of thinking about leitmotifs is to think about patterns of scenes. Freud seems largely out of fashion in psychology circles, but I believe his way of looking at character still has value for a novelist, in that things that happen to us when we are young get buried somewhere in our brains and play out in startling ways. Likewise, a scene with a character early in a novel can play out later in the book. Elena Ferrante's Neapolitan novels provide an excellent example of what I mean. Across four novels, starting with *My Brilliant Friend*, Ferrante tells the lifelong friendship of two women who grew up in a rough-and-tumble neighborhood in Naples. The narrator, Elena, gets out. She goes to high school, then college, then becomes a highly respected academic and novelist. Meanwhile, her friend Lila drops out of school, stays in Naples, marries and then leaves a thug, and has a comparably quiet, seemingly unhappy life (though the narrator's life is also not particularly happy, and her own marriage falls apart).

Over sixty years and 1200 pages, the two women have a strong, sometimes competitive, sometimes combative friendship, and the narrator in old age is still puzzling over who exactly her friend is. Lila is still a mystery, and the question goes unanswered: which one is ultimately the brilliant friend? The scholar who got out and became recognizably brilliant, or the poor local girl who was always a little quicker, a little bolder, and a little more insightful than the narrator? Early in the first novel, the two girls at eight years old have lost their dolls, and they have to go up the dank stairs to the home of Don Achille to ask him if they can get their dolls back. Don Achille is a Bad Dude, and the girls live in an environment of violence. It's a risk to go up there, yet Lila leads the way, and Elena follows. Then, a moment: "At the fourth flight Lila did something unexpected. She stopped to wait for me, and when I reached her she gave me her hand. This gesture changed everything between us forever."

That moment will follow them through the next thousand pages. Was Lila scared? Did she need Elena's hand as much as Elena needed hers? Or did she sense the fear in Elena, and intuit Elena would need a hand to keep going? I imagine that if Ferrante ever felt a little lost in her long narrative, ever wondered, "Who are these people anyway?" she could reread that scene, see the two girls in the dark stairway, one reaching out a hand for the other. An ambiguous gesture that changed everything between them. And then, I imagine, the author would feel grounded again and know exactly what her characters would do next. Although the reader might feel shock or dismay by Lila as she ages and hardens in the mean neighborhood of Naples, we never lose complete sympathy for her, because somewhere deep in our memory is this image of Lila, the scared or empathetic eight-year-old, reaching out to a friend, so when Lila lashes out or provides the cold shoulder, we know she may be afraid underneath the veneer, or have a goodness that is merely dormant.

Or maybe Lila was just having fun with Elena. After reading the four books, I still think Lila is something of a cipher. Like the narrator Elena, I can't quite put my finger on what she's about, which is what makes her interesting. A less satisfying novel would have clarified exactly who Lila is, assigned her a clear motivation, and given her a consistent identity. That may work with supporting characters—many fun, sparkly secondary characters hit only one note—but a main character needs some kind of complexity. Our consciousness is not fully unified. I think philosophers and neuroscientists alike would agree that while we feel like we have continuity of experience, continuity of memory, continuity of character, that sense of continuity is constructed— a story we assign ourselves to help the world make sense. A novelist working at the highest level intuits this process, and keeps her characters a little fuzzy. Remember Keats's praise of Shakespeare—that the bard had *negative capability*. Can we be certain we fully understand Hamlet's motivations? Why does he hesitate? And what about Iago? What is driving his villainy against Othello?

This quest to make sense of the world, to build a narrative around character, brings us from perspective to the next chapter on structure. Once you have your focal characters and you set them in motion in a scene, it's time to build a coherent story around them.

BUILDING THE STRUCTURE

Once you have set the scene and established your perspective, your next task is to connect a sequence of scenes and build out the novel. The broad issues are *handling time* and *telling a story*. There are a few craft terms pertinent to building the structure, including:

Summary refers to exposition that bridges two scenes or provides information outside of the current scene. Remember that a scene happens in real time, beat by beat, so summary conveys information outside of time. Let's say you have two characters having a conversation in a garage, and then you need to move them to a new setting later in the day. You might have a summary sentence: "They packed up the last of their things and brought them to the flea market, where they set up their wares and got ready to negotiate." This sentence brings us from the garage to the flea market, without having to give a scenic blow-by-blow of the drive over.

Back story and *flashbacks* refer to events that have happened before the current scene. Sometimes, you need to convey back story to explain something happening now (e.g., "He pulled off the freeway suddenly rather than continuing to drive behind a logging truck. When he was a teenager, he witnessed a log come off the back of a truck, and it almost impaled him"). That bit about the character as a teenager is back story, information conveyed in summary. A flashback would have fleshed out the back story as a scene.

One tip: Your natural inclination may be to layer in too much back story about your characters. Novels tend to start in the middle of the action, but when you do that you will have to fill in some contextual information. Just make sure you have a story that moves forward so that it's not all back story. I've read countless short story drafts in workshops where the author opens with a scene, and then has ten pages of back story, and then two pages of present-time narrative at the end. The balance is off, and if you only have a few pages of present-time scene, chances are the scene is under-baked or there isn't much of a story there.

Story and *plot* are sometimes used interchangeably; both generally refer to what happens in the course of a narrative. E.M. Forster gave a good example to differentiate them. He said a story might be: "The king died, and then the queen died." A plot might be: "The king died, and then the queen died of grief." Plot, for Forster, adds an element of causality, which I think you need in a novel. For me, a story is a sequence of events about a character or set of characters, and the sequence somehow conveys something meaningful. Your job as the novelist is to figure out what sequence of events need to be on the page, and in what order, to convey something meaningful.

Real life doesn't have much meaning in itself. We bounce around from day to day, we gradually change, and change again, and change again, and then we roll off this mortal coil. Just as a photographer will frame a picture, the novelist chooses certain events, a beginning and an ending, to create a story. Stories are what give our lives meaning, because they provide an understandable narrative with causality. Otherwise, we are like Job in the Bible, wandering around from one calamity to another without explanation. For example, I spent the first third of this book telling my story as a novelist. In the grand scheme of human affairs, this story doesn't mean anything. At all. But contextualized in a book about writing novels, written for people interested in such things, the story, I hope, has significance.

Story, then, is about context, and one major part of context is structure—how the narrative is framed. So, how do you structure your narrative?

To return to one default mode of contemporary American fiction—the third-person, past-tense, close or limited perspective—a novel is built from scenes. You get one scene, and then a space break or chapter break, and then you get another scene, and so on. Forty chapters later (about 300 pages), you have a novel.

In *Commonwealth*, Ann Patchett opens with the thirty-page party sequence around 1960. At the end of the sequence, Fix Keating tells Bert Cousins he should name his kid Albert. End chapter. Chapter two opens with a scene about fifty years later. Fix is an old man going through medical treatments, and he and his grown daughter are walking the halls of a hospital. Patchett doesn't give us any connective summary to get us there. She simply has a chapter break and then a new scene. Within chapter two, the dialogue and some judicious lines of back story clue us in on what we need to know—namely, that Fix and his wife divorced, Beverly married Bert, and the daughter grew up in a blended family. Scenes carry the story.

I don't know why scene is the dominant mode of fiction. Perhaps it's rooted in the history of narrative and the theater. Watching a play (or a movie), we get lost in the scenes, happening in real time before us. Likewise, scenes of a novel transport our minds in the same way, into the vivid and continuous dream. Big chunks of summary and other expository modes can be delightful to read, if you can get the voice right, but there's nothing like a scene to engage the reader. That's why I offered the tip above that it might be wise to limit back stories and flashbacks, to keep the reader grounded in the scene at hand. Likewise, you might be tempted to spend pages and pages describing the passage of time, but a space break or a chapter break can get the job done just as easily, so long as you are able to catch the reader up to speed in the next scene.

Hot tip: based on my experience as a novelist and from reading first novels from other writers, the temptation for inexperienced novelists is to spend too much energy on the passage of time, so we get pages and pages of a character driving around, or going through the weeks, where not much happens. My novel *The Whiskey Baron* originally took place over a year, and had plenty of passages of the cotton mill family going to work. In revision, I compressed the time of the novel to take place over about two weeks, which forced me to write in scene, which helped the pacing dramatically. If you have a novel to revise, consider compressing the timeline, or take a page out of Ann Patchett and just jump from one time to another without summary.

One excellent case study for handling time is Mohsin Hamid's *Exit West*. This novel is loosely based on the Syrian refugee crisis, and it follows a couple who are fleeing an unnamed Middle Eastern country in collapse. Before the collapse, the woman, Nadia, works for an insurance company, and the man, Saeed, is in branding. Then the bombings happen, and as their city collapses into a warzone, they realize they need to flee. The twist in this novel is that magical doors exist. The characters are able to walk through the door and be teleported to somewhere else. Nadia and Saeed arrange passage through several of these doors throughout the novel, arriving first in Greece and then in England and then in the United States. They can't control where they land, and they arrive sopping wet—much like the Syrian refugees washing up on the shores of Europe.

I can't say how Hamid came up with this conceit, but I'd bet it just popped into his head and sounded like a great idea: what if these refugees had a door they could teleport through? There's something surreal about the rapid collapse of a nation, so it makes sense to have a surreal element in such a novel. The magic trick, however, also serves a handy narrative function in that Hamid doesn't have to describe pages and pages of Nadia and Saeed in transit. They go through a door and, boom! They're in Greece. Boom! They're in England. Boom! They're in California. The first time they step through a magic door, Hamid gives us a space break and then:

> It was said in those days that the passage was both like a dying and like being born, and indeed Nadia experienced a kind of extinguishing as she entered the blackness and a gasping struggle as she fought to exit it, and she felt cold and bruised and damp as she lay on the floor of the room at the other side, trembling and too spent at first to stand, and she thought, while she strained to fill her lungs, that this dampness must be her own sweat.

That's such an economic way of handling the passage from their destroyed city to Europe. You can probably tell from the tone of the passage above that the prose sounds controlled, with a perspective psychically removed from the characters. The book overall reads like a fable or parable, which might grow tedious if it were 500 pages long, but my edition clocks in at 231 pages with wide margins, something you can read in a sitting or two. All the elements work together: the perspective is omniscient, bouncing between Saeed and Nadia but also commenting more broadly, like a fable. The story is rooted in scenes, with quick, surreal jumps in setting to keep the story tight. And the structure is a kind of quest, with the goal being freedom. It's also a love story that reaches a natural conclusion. In other words, it is a remarkable novel, all the more so for its brevity, the efficiency of the narrative.

Voice and perspective are strongly linked to time and structure. A retrospective first-person voice can bounce around in time as much as you want, so long as everything feels like it belongs and you ultimately build a pattern that makes sense. One of my favorite modes to read is an omniscient narrator, because this mode also allows a novel to bounce around in time, and it also allows for more liberal use of summary and back story.

The opening of Jonathan Franzen's *Freedom* is worth examining. The book is something of a throwback to the 19th century novel, an omniscient realist story in the mode of Dickens or Tolstoy. Plenty of novels make use of this mode—Richard Russo's *Empire Falls*, Min Jin Lee's *Pachinko*, Meg Wolitzer's *The Interestings*, Eleanor Caton's *The Luminaries*—but what I like about *Freedom* is it runs counter to a recommendation I made a few pages ago. The novel opens in 2004, when Walter Berglund is embroiled in some kind of a scandal. After a gossiping prologue, the novel gives us nearly 200 pages (40% of the novel) of his wife Patty's back story before returning to the present. That kind of extended flashback is a risk, but in this case it helps us get to know the characters fully, in a way that I think only the novel as an art form is capable of. The first paragraph sets the tone:

> The news about Walter Berglund wasn't picked up locally—he and Patty had moved away to Washington two years earlier and meant nothing to St. Paul now—but the urban gentry of Ramsey Hill were not so loyal to their city as not to read the *New York Times*. According to a long and very unflattering story in the *Times*, Walter had made quite a mess of his professional life out there in the nation's capital. His old neighbors had some difficulty reconciling the quotes about him in the *Times* ("arrogant," "high-handed," "ethically compromised") with the generous, smiling, red-faced 3M employee they remembered pedaling his commuter bicycle up Summit Avenue in February snow; it seemed strange that Walter, who was greener than Greenpeace and whose own roots were rural, should be in trouble now for conniving with the coal industry and mistreating country people. Then again, there had always been something not quite right about the Berglunds.

The perspective is not rooted with any one character in particular. Walter and Patty are clearly the center of the story, but this is a gossip mode, and indeed the prologue anchors us to a pair of neighbors, Seth and Merrie Paulson, who are incidental to the story but who serve as witnesses with the reader, giving us an insider-outsider's perspective.

The novel then has several pages of summary in this voice, and then we see Walter and Patty as a young couple gentrifying the neighborhood, and Franzen lists out a long list of questions (moral and otherwise) that run through Patty's head about their lives, the kind of things she might discuss with the neighbors:

> Was it better to offer panhandlers food, or nothing? Was it possible to raise unprecedentedly confident, happy, brilliant kids while working full-time? Could coffee beans be ground the night before you used them, or did this have to be done in the morning? Had anybody in the history of St. Paul ever had a positive experience with a roofer? What about a good Volvo mechanic? Did your 240 have that problem with the sticky parking-brake cable? And that enigmatically labeled dashboard switch that made such a satisfying Swedish click but seemed not to be connected to anything: what was that?
>
> For all queries, Patty Berglund was a resource, a sunny carrier of sociocultural pollen, an affable bee.

You can hear her voice here, Patty at a neighbor's house for cocktails or standing in the driveway while the kids motor around on bicycles, gossiping about minutia. Yet this voice is also ironic because it gives us a perspective on Patty that she wouldn't have for herself: the "affable bee."

Franzen then offers pages of summary interspersed with dialogue. An omniscient voice drops us in and out of quick scenes. For example, here's a quick flash of scene with Seth and Merry, who are chuckling over some woes of Patty and Walter's son, and Merrie says:

> "I'm sorry, it's just too funny and delicious. You'll have to do the non-gloating for the two of us and keep our fate at bay."
>
> "I feel bad for her."
>
> "Well, forgive me, but I'm finding it hilarious."

Toward the end of that winter, in Grand Rapids, Walter's mother collapsed with a pulmonary embolism on the floor of the ladies' dress shop where she worked.

There no space break or transition from the scene in dialogue to the next bit of summary about Walter's mother. The scenes are dropped in like accents, but the voice keeps moving through the story in that gossip, eavesdropping mode.

Henry James's metaphor for the structure of a novel was "architecture." In his preface to *The Portrait of a Lady*, he says, "The house of fiction has in short not one window, but a million—a number of possible windows not to be reckoned, rather; every one of which has been pierced, or is still pierceable, in its fast front, by the need of the individual vision and by the pressure of the individual will." In other words, there are a million ways to write a novel. Every novelist is looking out a different window, and your own vantage on the story will inform the kind of novel you build. In the next few pages, I'll tick through a few common ways to build the structure of a novel, but my strongest recommendation would be for you to look at your story and try to figure out what form you are working in. What other novels have been written that would sit well on the shelf with yours? Then take those other novels apart to figure out how they work and why. Close reading again.

The loosest form of novel, I would say, is the novel-in-stories, which is simply a collection of sequences (short stories) that create the pattern of a whole. In such novels, there's usually some kind of anchor—a common narrator, or a family, or an event that each story somehow comments on. Faulkner's *Go Down, Moses* is a series of stories about a family over generations. Is it a novel or a collection? Given Faulkner's obsession with history and the connection between the stories, I think it's most often viewed as a novel, but it's debatable. Colum McCann's *Let the Great World Spin* is almost universally considered a novel; it has a series of stories connected by an event, the day in 1974 when a tightrope walker walks out between the Twin Towers high in the clouds. What actually makes it a novel, other than the publisher's marketing? There are recurring patterns (or leitmotifs), as well as a few recurring characters, which give the book a unity of effect. But again, I wouldn't argue with someone who said the "novel" was really just a series of connected short stories.

Beyond unity of effect, what I look for in a novel is a plot, in Forster's definition, a causality that connects the sequence of events. Chapter one gives us the first flick of a domino, and the subsequent chapters spill out as a result of that first instigating event. In *Freedom*, the instigating event is what Franzen alludes to in the first chapter—a scandal in the heart of this ordinary American family. To justify why the scandal matters, we get several hundred pages of back story introducing us to the family, and then we witness the causal sequence of events from Patty's back story (her simultaneous, conflicted attraction to two men) to Walter's environmental catastrophe.

What's wrong at the beginning of the narrative? What question does the novel pose that needs to be answered by the end? And what is the causal sequence of events that connects the problem to the solution?

The standard structure is often an inverted checkmark pattern, sometimes called Freytag's pyramid: exposition, an instigating event, rising action, a climax, and then a resolution. The exposition is simply the who-what-where-when of the book as well as a statement of the problem. In *13 Ways of Looking at the Novel*, Jane Smiley suggests this occurs in the first 10% of the book, so one way of studying a novel is to find the 10% mark and then consider what information the author has given us at this point. Who are the characters? What has happened so far? And what dramatic incident happens around the 10% mark that starts the rising action?

Hamlet provides a good overview of this structure. In the beginning of the play, Hamlet is feeling kinda gloomy. He's a prince in Denmark, his father has died, and his mother, Gertrude, has remarried his uncle, Claudius, which Hamlet isn't happy about any of it. That's the who-what-where-when. The instigating event comes when he encounters the ghost of his father, who tells him he was murdered. Suddenly, we have the opening problem, or question. Was Hamlet's father murdered? Did Gertrude or Claudius murder him? Why? And, most importantly, what will Hamlet do about it?

For the next couple of acts, we see Hamlet wandering around ruminating on what he should do. He puts on a mask and pretends to be crazy with grief, which buys him some time to think. Should he seek vengeance? Confront his mother? He finally resolves to act, and he takes out his sword and kills…the wrong dude, a man named Polonius. The plot thickens, because now Hamlet can no longer pretend to be grief-crazy. There are consequences to the murder. Not only does Claudius intuit Hamlet knows the truth of his father's murder (and sends Hamlet off with Rosencrantz and Guildenstern to be murdered), but Polonius's son Laertes wants vengeance against Hamlet as well. The instigating event (the ghost of old Hamlet) causes one event after another until the climactic duel between Hamlet and Laertes.

The story is more complicated than what I just outlined, but the drama is ultimately causal in nature. From the appearance of the ghost in Act 1, Hamlet can no longer do nothing. He must act, and his sequence of actions have effects which lead to further actions and ultimately to nearly everyone's death.

To me, the mystery genre provides the clearest structure for a novel. As a character tells the detective in the TV show *Bosch*, based on Michael Connelly's novels, "I envy the clarity of your mission, Bosch. Somebody's dead, and somebody did it." The structure is that a dead body shows up in the beginning, someone comes out to investigate the murder, and at the end the killer is unveiled and brought to justice. Within this structure, the mystery novel offers a great deal of wiggle room, and my interest in the form is often less "who" dunnit but rather "how" the mystery will be solved. Detectives, spies, reporters, and other sleuths who solve mysteries are interesting characters to spend time with in a novel because they are great observers of people. They often have some special insight into the world and human nature, so watching the operation of their minds is enjoyable.

A good example is Louise Penny's first novel, *Still Life*, which is the first a long series around Chief Inspector Armand Gamache. The Canadian village of Three Pines, south of Montreal, provides the kind of cloistered community you need in a certain type of mystery: a small village, a large country house, an island. Trapping a small cast of characters in a place is one common structural device for many genres, not just mystery. To name a few: *Moby-Dick* (a boat), Thomas Mann's *The Magic Mountain* (a sanitarium), Ann Patchett's *Bel Canto* (a compound that terrorists have taken over), Ken Kesey's *One Flew Over the Cuckoo's Nest* (a mental institution), Michael Crichton's *Sphere* (an underwater Navy installation) and *Jurassic Park* (an island overrun by dinosaurs), and any number of Agatha Christie novels—*Murder on the Orient Express* (a train), *And Then There Were None* (an estate on a private island), *Peril at End House* (a resort), and so forth.

Penny opens *Still Life* with the murder of one Jane Neal, an elderly woman shot by an arrow in the woods on Thanksgiving. Three Pines is a place without much crime, so locals assume it must have been a hunting accident. Montreal Chief Inspector Gamache comes in with his team (his right-hand man, Jean, and a newbie on the force, Yvette), and soon begins to suspect something more at play than a mere hunting accident.

The novel is about 300 pages, and in the first 10%, we meet half a dozen core members of the close-knit community, and we see a scene with Jane in flashback. We also meet Gamache and his team, and see them getting the call about the dead woman in Three Pines. So, they gather together and make the trek out. When Gamache begins to treat it as a serious murder inquiry, it puts the town on edge, and we get to see how some of the characters act under pressure—an easy way to get to know someone. Finally, we witness an underlying tension in Gamache's team due to some scandal that he was privy to in the past, as well as friction with Yvette as the new member on the team. Unlike *Hamlet*, in which the falling dominos center on what decision Hamlet will make, the dominos in *Still Life* center around the investigation.

Who do you investigate first? Well, they start with a man named Ben, Jane's friend who found the body (in mysteries, there's a good chance that the person who found the body is also the killer). Then they look to the family who stands to inherit some money, another common culprit. We watch Gamache and his team get to know the townspeople and the village itself. While they are conducting interviews, they send an arrow stuck in a tree off for forensics analysis. Being this far out of Montreal, they don't have a CSI team on hand. It's not that kind of novel. The detective is left to his own devices, an old-fashioned approach to a mystery. The novel was published in 2005, before smart phones and social media shrank the world. If Penny wrote it today and set it in 2020, she would need to update a good bit of the investigation to match technology—a growing challenge for today's mystery novelist.

The pleasure from the novel is partly about who the killer is, but it's also about inhabiting the world of Three Pines, where life moves at a little slower pace. It's the kind of place you might want to live yourself, where people are friendly and kind, and they gather at the local café, and more or less everyone gets along as friends. Then there's Gamache himself, who bears a strong resemblance to Christie's detective Hercule Poirot—late middle aged, quiet, polite, decent, but deceptively sharp. He's a man we trust and are rooting for:

> Armand Gamache sat on the bench, watching the birds but mostly watching the village. Before his eyes the village of Three Pines seemed to slow right down. The insistence of life, the bustle and energy became muffled. The voices dropped, gaits slowed. Gamache sat back and did what he did best. He watched. He took in the people, their faces, their actions, and where possible he took in what they said, though people stayed far enough away from his wooden bench on the grass that he couldn't hear much. He noticed who touched and who didn't. Who hugged and who shook hands. He noticed who had red eyes and who gave the appearance of business as usual.

In many ways, Gamache is a straightforward, even predictable investigator, but his mind is nevertheless an entertaining place to spend your time, because as he is noticing things about people, we start to notice them too. Reading about a detective turns the reader into a detective, which is fun.

Unlike some mysteries, Penny's novel floats around in point of view (third person limited, roving by section or chapter to different characters), so we get to know Gamache's new trainee, Yvette, who is ambitious and eager to be working with the legendary detective. When he doesn't immediately see her brilliance, her admiration quickly turns to petty jealousies and backstabbing, which creates a subplot in the book. Most mysteries have a subplot, wherein the sleuth has something else going on in their world that is hounding them while they are trying to solve the case at hand. In the case of *Still Life*, Agent Yvette becomes a problem for Gamache, and then over the next few books in the series, she ties in with the mysterious scandal in his past.

We also get to know Clara Morrow, a local artist and a kind soul who serves as the moral center of Three Pines in all of the Gamache novels. At the end of the book, Clara hosts a party that features some of Jane's last artwork, a painting about the town history, and she notices a piece of the painting has been altered. That leads her and Gamache to the killer, who was also, it turns out, responsible for the death of another townsperson before the novel opened. The villain killed the first victim (whose death had appeared natural) out of a desire for money, but then killed Jane because she knew and had put a clue about the murder in her painting about the town history. That's something else mysteries have in common: a second murder. Agatha Christie was the queen of this: murder number one brings out the detective (Hercule Poirot or Miss Marple), and just when they think they might be getting close to solving the case, another murder happens right in time to complicate things. Often, the prime suspect ends up murdered, sending them back to square one.

Jane Smiley has several handy rules of thumb around structure. She says the exposition takes place over the first 10% of the novel, and the climax and denouement happen around the

85-90% mark. She also notes that something interesting usually happens around the 60% mark. The middle of a book tends to sag, so often an author will do something to spice things up a little more than halfway through. In an Agatha Christie novel, the prime suspect might get murdered around the 60% mark. In *Still Life*, the detectives receive DNA results which send them back to the victim's family member as the prime suspect. He ends up being innocent, but on page 183 out of 312, the DNA results sound promising, like Gamache is homing in on the killer. The 60% mark is a great spot for a red herring or misdirection.

Suffice to say we have met the real killer already, and most probably dismissed him (or her) through the author's sleight of hand. Other suspects appear more probable—possibly this family member whose DNA matches an arrow in the woods—but it takes the investigation to uncover the *why*, which leads to the *who*. I won't spoil the ending, but form and function meet beautifully: the small-town mystery has at its core the small-town relationships. The *why* matters less than the *who*, and the *who* matters because of *how* it disrupts the nature of the town. The novel has two problems in the beginning: first, who killed Jane and why? Second, is this small town safe? The investigation has taken us through the rising action to the climactic answer. By uncovering the killer (the who), and the why, order is restored. The end gives us the answer to the mystery but also implies the town is, indeed, safe.

One final novel I'd like to look at for structure is Philip Roth's *The Ghost Writer*, which would be an excellent book for any young novelist to read simply to better understand the creative process. Roth more than anyone since Henry James has embedded the process of writing a novel into his novels themselves. I might even suggest *The Ghost Writer*, *Counterlife*, and *American Pastoral* provide a better blueprint for how to be a novelist than any craft book you can find.

Examining the book from the outside, *The Ghost Writer* is a slim volume. My copy is 180 pages, 40,000 words or so, a very short novel. It's broken into four parts: (1) Maestro, (2) Nathan Dedalus, (3) Femme Fatale, and (4) Married to Tolstoy, which brings to mind the structure of a symphony. One of the best reads on Roth, in my opinion, is Claudia Pierpont Roth's biography *Roth Unbound*. In it, she reads *The Ghost Writer* as a symphony with part three being a "scherzo," a musical form commonly translated as "joke." You'll see why in a moment. She also reads the novel as a *küntslerroman*, which refers to a book about the development of an artist. The form is similar to the *bildungsroman*, which is the fancy German word for coming-of-age novel. The novel is Roth's first novel in a series narrated by his alter-ego character, Nathan Zuckerman. The novel opens:

> It was the last daylight hour of a December afternoon more than twenty years ago—I was twenty-three, writing and publishing my first short stories, and like many a *Bildungsroman* hero before me, already contemplating my own massive *Bildungsroman*—when I arrived at his hideaway to meet the great man. The clapboard farmhouse was at the end of an unpaved road twelve hundred feet up in the Berkshires, yet the figure who emerged from the study to bestow a ceremonious greeting wore a gabardine suit, a knitted blue tie clipped to a white shirt by an unadorned silver clasp, and well-brushed ministerial black shoes that made me think of him stepping down from a shoeshine rather than from the high altar of art.

What do we make of this from a craft perspective? It's in the first person, telling a story twenty years ago, so the psychic distance is somewhat removed. Our narrator, whom we soon enough find out is Nathan Zuckerman, is erudite and holds capital-L Literature in the highest esteem. His hero, E.I. Lonoff, is wearing "ministerial" shoes; Literature is Nathan's church, and Lonoff is his minister. We also suspect this novel is, in fact, the *bildungsroman* he hints he will one day write. We are reading his coming-of-age story that he was only beginning to contemplate. In other words, the novel is something of a metafiction, a novel about the making of fiction.

Structurally, the novel takes place over twenty-four hours in the present, with flashbacks to Nathan's past. Part one is tells the story of this evening, when he meets with Lonoff, Lonoff's wife, Hope, and a young woman living with them, Amy Bellette. After this opening paragraph, we get a little back story about Nathan and how he ended up here, before getting to the meat of his meeting with the great writer. The sequence carries us to page 73, a fine example of economy of scene. By economy, I mean Roth packs all the story into a short period of time; he keeps the novel tightly, almost claustrophobically, focused on this one evening.

Plot-wise, what is wrong at the beginning of this novel? What question needs to be answered? This doesn't have a clear problem like a murder mystery, but I suppose the question is, will Nathan get what he needs out of Lonoff? Are we in fact reading the *bildungsroman* he was setting out to write? Does the minister of Literature bless him so that he will be able to find his individual talent?

In part one, Nathan and Lonoff discuss books, and Nathan grows more and more curious about the girl living with them. She is young, yet he finds out she is not Lonoff's daughter: "Who is she then, being served snacks by his wife on the floor of his study? His concubine? Ridiculous, the word, the very idea, but there it was obscuring all other reasonable and worthy thoughts." This question of the girl's identity pops up on page 21 of my edition, just past the 10% mark. One might read it as the instigating event, the moment the rising action occurs. Nathan's original problem was getting blessed by the minister of Literature, but his new problem is figuring out who this girl's identity is. A few pages later, we learn she is formerly a student who is now helping Lonoff organize his manuscripts. When she speaks, "Miss Bellette's speech was made melodious by a faint foreign accent." Who *is* she?

After Amy takes off, Nathan, Lonoff and his wife have dinner and discuss many things. Among them, we learn Amy is a refugee from somewhere in Europe. Then, Lonoff and his wife get into an argument. Later in the evening, Lonoff praises Nathan's work, which sends Nathan into ecstasy. He retires to his room exhilarated.

In part two, we get a great deal of back story about Nathan, and his arguments with his father over his chosen a career as a writer. In Lonoff's guest room, he tries to compose a letter to his father, to explain and justify himself. One rift between father and son is that Nathan has rejected his family and his Jewish heritage, to some degree, at least enough that his mother feels the need to ask him if he is himself anti-Semitic. The section's title, "Nathan Dedalus," is a clear reference to James Joyce's Stephen Dedalus, who in *A Portrait of the Artist as a Young Man* rejects his own Irish Catholic upbringing and moves to continental Europe to pursue life as an artist. Late in the evening, Amy returns to the house, and soon Nathan hears a thud in the room above him. He stands on a chair to eavesdrop (as any good writer would) and overhears a melodramatic conversation between Amy and Lonoff.

Part three is the magic trick of the novel, the "scherzo." The point of view shifts to third person, and Roth treats us to Amy's story, or Nathan's imagined version of Amy's story, answering the question about her that has been raised this evening:

> It was only a year earlier that Amy had told Lonoff her whole story. Weeping hysterically, she had phoned him one night from the Biltmore Hotel in New York; as best he could understand, that morning she had come down alone on a train from Boston to see the matinee performance of a play, intending to return home again by train in the evening. Instead, after coming out of the theater she had taken a hotel room, where ever since she had been "in hiding."

In Nathan's imagined narrative, Amy Bellette is Anne Frank, having survived the Bergen-Belsen concentration camp and made her way to the United States. Only, by the time she emerges, her diary has been discovered and made public. She has become a public face of the Holocaust, and her diary and the tragedy of her death has captured the mind of the world. She now feels a responsibility to remain "dead," in hiding, so that the public figure of Anne Frank may live on as symbol against the forces of the Holocaust.

Roth presents this section straight, as if it is the real narrative and Amy is in fact Anne Frank, but we know it is a story Nathan has written down after being inspired by the evening. He is a fiction writer, after all, and his job is to make up stories. What's interesting about *The Ghost Writer* is that in giving us Nathan's story within the story, Roth shows us how the mind of a novelist works. We see the clues from parts one and two that Nathan is growing obsessed with Amy Bellette's character, which is one way a novel begins—with an abiding image, and then a question. Amy Bellette: who is she? Then, Roth shows us the mask of Nathan Zuckerman, narrating an omniscient story about Amy as Anne Frank. In the chapter on perspective, I said the third person limited and omniscient modes had an outside narrator, separate from the character and usually unacknowledged. In *The Ghost Writer*, Roth gives us the narrator—Nathan—and spends three-quarters of the book developing him. Only in this third part, "Femme Fatale," do we get a traditional story with a narrator unacknowledged in the section—but of course we know who the narrator is. Since we know his predilections and his complicated relationship with his family and his heritage, we see where the story of Amy as Anne came from.

In an interview, Roth discussed his revision process for this novel. He said he had trouble writing the Anne Frank sections in third person because he kept idolizing her in the prose, holding her up on a pedestal. To solve the problem, he re-wrote the section into first-person, which he said allowed him to write her story more directly and honestly. He then translated the first-person version back into third, replacing I's with she's and such, and this process fixed the issue of voice.

Part four brings us back to Nathan's perspective. The next morning over breakfast, Hope gets into an argument with Amy and Lonoff, and then she storms off down the road. Nathan helps Lonoff into his coat so Lonoff can go after his wife, but before he goes, Lonoff says,

> "You had an earful this morning."
> I shrugged. "It wasn't so much."

"So much as what, last night?"

"Last night?" Then does he know all I know? But what *do* I know, other than what I can imagine?

"I'll be curious to see how we all come out someday. It could be an interesting story. You're not so nice and polite in your fiction," he said. "You're a different person."

"Am I?"

"I should hope so."

The novel never really gives us an answer about Amy Bellette's character. We are in Nathan's head, and as he acknowledges here on the last page, all he knows is what he can imagine. He imagines her as Anne Frank, but that's all we as the reader can know as well. We do, however, get the answer to the novel's other opening question. Here, Nathan has gotten the blessing from the minister of Literature. Lonoff gives him permission to write the story, which gives him permission to call himself a Writer. By eavesdropping on his host and then writing the story of Amy as Anne, Nathan has earned the blessing he came for.

And we, the readers, are treated to an inside look at the mind of a novelist. We see where stories come from, and how a novelist executes. We see the importance of doubt when Nathan asks, "But what *do* I know, other than what I can imagine?" There is one additional literary reference running through *The Ghost Writer*, which is that Nathan loves Henry James's story "The Middle Years," and he references a quote from that story. James writes, "We work in the dark—we do what we can—we give what we have. Our doubt is our passion, and our passion is our task. The rest is the madness of art."

That is a fine motto for anyone interested in the art and craft of being a novelist.

ON REVISION & RESPONSIBILITY

I don't know what to say about revision. Some book people make a fetish of it, saying things like "all writing is re-writing," or glorifying the number of drafts their novel went through, or unpacking the word "re-vision," creating a "new vision" or "re-envisioning" the work. These same voices make it sound as though you must revise, and revise radically, for your novel to succeed.

It's certainly part of the job, but I would caution that every book is different, and every writer is different. My novels *The Whiskey Baron* and *The Edge of America* went through some extensive re-envisioning over many years. I wrote them using the process I outlined earlier in this section, exploring scenes and characters and taking the narrative down tangents. To use a pottery analogy, the first drafts were like a lump of clay, and revision was a matter of breaking down and then shaping and re-shaping the pot. This is what the poet Richard Hugo called "the triggering town"—you start with one thing in mind, and then somewhere along the way you take a leap to something else. Jonathan Franzen reportedly started *The Corrections* as another "systems novel" in the vein of his first two books, but after following a character around for years, he eventually latched onto an elderly couple, who had shown up tangentially, and wrote the entire novel about them.

As I've gotten older and more experienced, my first drafts are much closer to the final. The books still need *editing*, of course, but I think I'm spending more time reflecting on the story and characters up front, moving into a book more slowly, so that the first draft is more fully realized. The language of product development may be a useful analogy. When company researchers decide to innovate a new product, they'll put a bunch of people in a room for a discovery phase. They'll throw ideas on the wall and brainstorm and generally think about what the product could do, what it would look like, and what the market for it would be. Then, engineers or developers will start making something. They'll iterate on a design to create a prototype, or perhaps what's called a "minimum viable product." From there, they'll put it out in front of consumers so they can test and refine and write a business plan for the product. They'll refine it over a few stages before finally launching it into the world.

So, the phases are, roughly, the concept/discovery phase, the development phase, and the testing/marketing phase. For my first novels I wrote out scenes while in the discovery phase. I like that approach because, to me, writing something down makes it real in a way that merely thinking about it does not. My revision process was therefore the equivalent of the development phase, shaping a novel to be as good as I could make it. I'd send it out to a few friends, and then to agents, and that process was something like the marketing phase of product development. Now, my process is to think about a book for longer, so that the first draft is akin to the development phase, meaning the first draft is farther along the product development chute. It's not a perfect analogy, but you get the idea. There's no universal rule for how to get the job done. Maybe you need one draft and some editing, or maybe you need fifty drafts. Either way, your readers will only see the final product.

Because readers are only privy to published work, the revision process remains somewhat mysterious. We, the reading public, only know what authors choose to tell us. Edward P. Jones has said in interviews that he carried the characters from *The Known World* around in his head for years, but that when he finally sat down to write the novel, he was able to bang it out in a year or two. Meanwhile, my friend Virginia Pye has discussed the process that led to her first novel, *River of Dust*. Apparently, she'd worked for years on a multi-generation family saga that lacked structure. An editor nudged her into focusing the novel on one discreet event—the kidnapping of a child—and she was able to plot out and write the novel in a matter of weeks. Both Pye and Jones went through a discovery phase, a phase of deep thinking and rumination. Jones kept it in his head, whereas Pye wrote hers down, but when they each reached the end of that phase, they were able to write their novels swiftly, with what sounds like minimal big-picture revisions.

I have no advice for how to revise a book, or how to know when a book is finished. I suspect you know, on some level, whether the story is as good as you can make it, or if something is lingering in your brain. In his book *On Writing*, Stephen King says he will let his first draft sit for six weeks or so, enough time for the story to grow cold, and then he will reread it to start his revision. I usually need longer than six weeks for a story to grow cold. In fact, I like to write a first draft of something new—or at least have an idea for something new—because a shiny new novel in the works helps me approach an old novel more dispassionately, and therefore more honestly.

That's what you want: an honest assessment of the work.

The question of revision is strongly linked to the question of audience. Who or what are you writing for? If you are writing for a commercial audience—to gain readers, earn praise, maybe even make a living—your job is to entertain, to be *the* choice for how consumers spend their time.

I worry about the purely commercial novelist. If you designed an AI system to write a purely commercial novel, a focus-tested consumer product, there's a decent chance the system will produce something insidious. Humans have base instincts, so we may be drawn to a dangerous drug over a nourishing choice. A flavor chemist once told me that we have very few receptors to sense sugar compared to other flavors, which is why we get such a neurochemical hit from sugar. A consumer-driven flavor chemist, then, might go to work for a candy company to create a sugary product as addictive as nicotine, something with no redeeming value, and the market would reward such an endeavor.

What might the nicotine-candy version of a story look like? Consider the case of the writer Nasdijj, a pseudonym for an author who published three critically acclaimed "memoirs" about his life as a Navajo in the early 2000s. It turns out, the man behind the pseudonym was a white writer named Tim Barrus, and he was cashing in on the market for multicultural memoirs (and memoirs in general; this was the same era that James Frey embellished his own memoir with falsehoods). It was unethical for Barrus to construct Nasdijj, but not all that surprising. After all, from a commercial stance, he was giving audiences what they wanted, and many of his readers were no doubt moved by his stories. Does the fact that they were fiction negate the experience those readers had? Where does an author's responsibility lie? Is the novelist's job simply to entertain, or is there a moral obligation beyond telling a good story? I hope most of us would say that Barrus/Nasdijj is a scourge, but I would add that he was enabled by the system around him, a publisher who didn't dig too deeply into his identity, readers hungry for a certain kind of story, media with an appetite to promote such a story, and a free market that allowed his literary career to flourish, at least until the hoax was revealed in 2006.

Since then, as our media has become more fragmented, niche markets are serving up stories designed to make us feel good about ourselves and our worldview. Stories are successful because they have the power to create a sense of community, which I think we are all looking for on some level. A connection to another human being. A sense of belonging. If I make a joke, we both laugh at the same punchline. We're in communion with each other, in a micro-community. Expand that notion, and consider the Hebrew Bible, which was largely composed during the Babylonian Captivity. While in exile from Jerusalem, the Judeans systematically composed the stories to define their community as descendants of Abraham. The act of storytelling created the Judean community when they no longer had a nation to call home. Fast forward to the 21st century, and what are our central stories? Some Americans have fallen back on nationalism, or tribal identities. Others are finding identity through media narratives. You can go through your day and get one reality from Twitter and the Daily Kos, or you can get a completely different reality from Facebook and the Drudge Report. Such an environment is how conspiracies thrive: the idea that 9/11 was an inside job, or that vaccines cause autism.

Stories have great power, and therefore I believe storytellers have the responsibility to interrogate their work—to fully understand what they are saying, and their own motivations for saying it. If writing is an act of discovery, then you discover what you have to say about the world through writing. Or, as Don DeLillo put it, "Writing is a concentrated form of thinking."

I'm not arguing that storytellers have a responsibility to write moral fiction, or to remain faithful to their tribe, or anything like that, but I am arguing you have a responsibility to understand what you are putting down on the page. I once sat in a writers workshop where a white author referenced a black character in a somewhat racist manner—perhaps employing dialect around the black character that clearly set the character off as an "other." The author in these cases had what is known as "unconscious bias," a blind spot in his own character, or his own assumptions about who he was writing for (i.e., other white readers). The class had to gently discuss the racism of the character while the author grew red in the face as it dawned on him that we all thought he was a racist. Just as poker players have tells that communicate something about their hand, fiction writers also have tells, elements of the prose that communicate something about their characters or intentions or assumptions.

Dialect is an easy example to point to. If you go back a generation, it's easy to find books by white authors in which the central characters speak in a standard English with standard spelling, but a non-white character (or sometimes a rural or poor character) speaks in dialect, with orthographic changes to emphasize the "otherness" of the speech. That technique makes an assumption about who the reader is—namely, the reader is a person like the author, white and educated, someone who, like the author, would hear the dialect as being "other." It's a subtle kind of racism, but the author could be making the unconscious assumption of a bond between herself and the reader as being one kind of person (white, educated), different from the speaker in dialect (possibly poor, uneducated, or non-white). The answer isn't to forego using dialect in fiction completely (though I would argue against orthographic changes, and I would argue that a little bit of dialect goes a long way). The answer is to recognize what you are doing, and to examine the patterns of which characters speak in dialect and which ones do not, and to ask yourself what assumptions you are making about your reader.

As I write this book, in early 2020, Jeanine Cummins's novel *American Dirt* has just been released, accompanied by controversy. The novel tells the story of a Mexican migrant on the run to America, and the publisher and the majority of early reviewers have praised the book to high heaven as a "*Grapes of Wrath* for our time." Oprah even selected it for her book club on its release day. Meanwhile, many writers on Twitter took the novel to task for being both badly written and an act of cultural appropriation— trauma porn, a story profiting off the inaccurate and stereotypical portrayal of Mexicans. The controversy around the book is amplifying a broader conversation around the #OwnVoices movement, a push within publishing to promote writers from marginalized communities to tell their own stories, stories that historically have been told by white writers. Some of the political push in that movement has interrogated whether you have any right to write about someone outside your community—for instance, a white writer inhabiting the mind of a non-white character. Cummins, it seems, has failed to get the details right and therefore has produced a nicotine-candy story for a primarily white audience.

As a straight white male writer, I don't really have the standing to comment on the #OwnVoices movement and what you can and can't do as a fiction writer. I believe writers have the creative license to enter the minds of people unlike themselves, but I also believe doing so comes with responsibility to the people you're representing, to get the details right. What the conversation around *American Dirt* has brought up, for me, is the fundamental fact that stories lie—that stories, in essence, *are* lies. A story, by definition, is framed through a perspective, a beginning and an ending. The storyteller omits anything outside the frame, thus creating a fiction, a lie. Sometimes lies illuminate a greater truth. Other times, the lies are simply there to sell you something—a product, an election, a point of view. The credible reader won't know which is which, a good lie or a malicious lie. Truth is subjectivity, and it could be many readers' truth to be moved by *American Dirt*, same as many readers were moved by Nasdijj before he was revealed to be a fraud.

The fallout from *American Dirt* has been dispiriting, to say the least. So many prominent writers and booksellers have latched onto the question of who can tell what story, and reduced the controversy to one of censorship. These voices have said the writing is enough, and reading *American Dirt*, they know what they know. What they miss is that—as with the case of Nasdijj—sometimes the text itself isn't enough.

Stories are lies, so therefore it is the storyteller's (and the publisher's) responsibility to do your due diligence. Approach the material with sensitivity, and admit your own blind spots. Come to the page with a stance of *I know nothing*. Recent years have also seen the rise of "sensitivity readers," which I think is mis-branded, given the connotation between "sensitivity" and what some might dismiss as "liberal snowflake sensibility." The role of an "accuracy reader," however, is critical. You owe it to your readers, and to yourself, to get the details right, whether it's a white person writing about a Mexican migrant, a New Yorker writing about Eastern Kentucky, or a non-veteran writing about war. Otherwise, you risk exploitation. It's hard enough to get the details of our own lives right, so the challenge is even greater when writing about something outside our immediate purview.

I would point to the writer Alexander Chee as a serious voice in this conversation. In an essay for *Vulture*, he outlined three questions he has for a novelist interested in writing a character from a different background:

- Why do you want to write from this character's point of view?
- Do you read writers from this community currently?
- Why do you want to tell this story?

His questions get at the heart of where writers go wrong, not just in writing about characters of a different race or ethnicity, but in writing fiction at large. You would do well, in your revision process, to answer these questions about all of your characters. Chee writes,

> I once advised a young white writer who believed that because she had loved a novel written by a writer from a certain background that she, too, could write about a family from that background. Her country had colonized this country, but a condition of being a colonizer is that you do not know the country you are taking possession of, or the culture—you don't have to. I knew the questions this student still had to answer because I knew people from this community. I had to draw her attention to everything she didn't know. She seemed resentful throughout.

Everything she didn't know. Unconscious bias. Blind spots. Ignorance. These are the things you will constantly run up against as a fiction writer. While I still believe fiction writers can do anything they want, the best advice I can offer is to approach any story you write with a sense of humility. Curiosity. Openness. Negative capability. Fiction is about getting outside your own head, but doing so honestly, authentically, and responsibly is a much taller order than it might seem.

Why do you want to write this particular story? And why are you the best person to tell this story? I think the answer has to involve your own story, and the way your worldview is embedded in the story. Book people online love to make fun of Jonathan Franzen as being part of the old guard, the old privileged white male writer, but I suspect he would agree with Chee's questions to ask yourself. In a list of "10 Rules for Novelists," published on *Lit Hub*, Franzen writes, "The most purely autobiographical fiction requires pure invention. Nobody ever wrote a more auto-biographical story than *The Metamorphosis*." I believe what he meant is that in the story of Gregor Samsa waking up as a bug, Kafka shows us the world according to Franz Kafka. *The Metamorphosis* is a fiction, but Kafka is personally embedded in the story. Through this lens, perhaps all fiction is autobiographical to some degree, so whatever subject matter you choose, you should probably be able to find your own personal stakes in the story.

The market may reward you for bulldozing over capital-T Truth with a good story, but here at the end of the craft section of this book, I'll return once again to James Baldwin's comment: "People pay for what they do, and still more for what they have allowed themselves to become, and they pay for it very simply: by the lives they lead." Baldwin was specifically writing about white Americans and their oppression of black Americans. He was arguing white oppressors would pay for their actions simply by the fact of existing as oppressors. You are who you are, no matter what material rewards the world is giving you. I would recommend you write that quote on an index card and hang it on your wall during revision. When you are ready to call your book done, consider what it means for you to have written it. Is it your best work? Is it generous in spirit? Is it a story that only you could tell? Can you find yourself and your own life in the story? Did you learn anything?

I believe Curtis Sittenfeld said something to the effect that if you feel like something is wrong with a book but you don't know how to fix it, it's okay to let it go, but if you know how to fix it and just don't want to put in the work, you better sit down and do the work. It all comes back to doing the work: drafting the novel, and then revising it to the best of your abilities, and then finding someone you can trust to read it and give you an honest assessment, and then giving your own honest assessment, and then continuing to work until you've exhausted every tool at your disposal.

And then, it's onto the free market.

THE BUSINESS

INSIDE BASEBALL

Brace yourself.

This isn't going to be pretty. In part one, I circled around and around the book business. I talked about the glut of writers coming out of MFA programs, the paucity of teaching gigs, and the struggle with reconciling yourself to your own abilities. Again and again, I returned to the idea of luck. The good fortune of having the right book at the right time and getting it on the right editor's desk. There's also an entire industry to contend with. A business that includes everything from rights management to a supply and distribution chain to profit-and-loss statements. If you want to be a professional novelist, you will be inside this system, and therefore you would be well served to understand how it works from the inside out.

I should say that I am still learning about this industry. I opened the LLC for Haywire Books more than a year ago, and I am constantly stumbling onto new information and new perspectives on the publishing business. I once heard a sales rep say on a panel that the most important thing to understand about the book business is that it's not a business. By that she meant it didn't operate the way most businesses do, and therefore it contains pitfalls and opportunities that your average business-person doesn't have to contend with.

I should also say that when I started Haywire Books, I'd published (and signed contracts) for a dozen stories in magazines as well as one novel with a traditional publisher. I'd been in this business for years, yet I have been astounded by how little I knew about the world I was a part of. You might think running a small press is about finding great manuscripts and ushering books into the world, but most of it is about discount codes and shipping rates.

This final section is going to offer a big-picture summary of what this business is about, how an author fits in, where the money comes from and goes, and what's changing now that we're deep into the 21st century. This information likely won't—and shouldn't—affect what you write and how you approach your craft, but it might change what you decide to do with your book when it's finished. Traditional versus self-publishing. To query agents or go it alone. To try to get the Big Splashy Debut, or stay under the radar for a few books. You have choices, but every time you walk through one door, another door closes.

RIGHTS

Let's start with the product you are selling. A novel is a piece of intellectual property, and when you sell a novel, you are selling the intellectual property "rights" for someone else to publish, distribute, and sell it in various formats. Rights are traditionally packaged and sold by format: hardback, trade paperback, mass-market paperback, e-book, audio book, and so forth. Each edition is a different kind of right.

Then, there are subsidiary rights, which generally refer to a second level of packaging and sales. These may include foreign rights (sold for translation to different markets), movie rights, merchandising rights, and the like. If a book becomes a runaway bestseller, it may eventually become a Brand with all kinds of stuff associated with it. Think about Harry Potter, which was originally a series of books but now includes a series of films, a theme park, lines of merchandise, and various other commercial worlds. You and I can't go out and sell Harry Potter t-shirts or wizard wands without infringing on J.K. Rowling's intellectual property rights. That's what she created when she created the world of Harry Potter. A world of intellectual property.

Most books don't become Brands like that. Most novels sell in a few formats (hardback, paperback, e-book, and audio book), with maybe a foreign sale or a movie option as kind of a lucky bonus. Your first customer is the publisher, who might buy "all world rights" or something like that. The publisher will register the copyright in your name, and then they will purchase the rights to do something with your intellectual property (i.e., package it as a book and sell it). They'll also try to sell the subsidiary rights, in which a foreign publisher or a Hollywood studio will then buy the rights to do something else with the work (i.e., translate it and sell it, or turn it into a movie script).

You as the author benefit from this system because every time a new right is used, you get paid. Books are seldom profitable when they are sold as one format, but when you can package and re-sell the same product again and again, it can become very profitable. The challenge, of course, is how to sell it again and again. Your first-stop publisher may do so some of that, or if you have an agent, they might negotiate with the publisher to sell some of the rights while leaving the rest in a pool to sell separately.

If you're negotiating your own contracts, one thing to look for is a "rights reversion" clause. A publisher might buy all world rights, but with a rights reversion clause, you get your rights back after a certain period of time if the publisher hasn't done anything with them. What you don't want is for some publisher to buy all your rights and sit on them forever, because that will limit you in the future.

I'm not an attorney, so my best recommendation, if you are offered a publishing contract, is to have an attorney look it over. If you have an agent, she or he will negotiate the contract on your behalf, but I still might recommend an independent attorney look over the contract.

Literary Agents

The author and the reader might be the only two players who ultimately matter in the book business, because there is no business without them, but there is an enormous supply and distribution chain of middlemen that are worth understanding if you want to be a professional novelist: agents, publishers, the media, and all the people in the book trade (distributors, wholesalers, retailers).

If you're going through the traditional publishing route, your first stop will likely be a literary agent, who acts as a representative to sell your book to a major publisher. Like a real estate agent, a literary agent works on commission, and usually takes 15% of what they sell. Plenty has been written online about how to find an agent, how to make a pitch, and generally what the agent-author dynamic is like. The websites agentquery.com (free) or Publishers Marketplace (small monthly fee) are pretty good resources for introductory information.

A few shades of nuance I will add:

First, agents definitely play a critical role in traditional publishing. As an author, you almost certainly will not get a book deal with a big-five New York publisher, see a five-figure advance, get reviewed in the *New York Times* or the *Washington Post* or *Entertainment Weekly*, or sell the movie rights to your book without an agent.

However.

Agents are not the only way to get your career going.

If you have a book you think has commercial potential, by all means try to get an agent. When you do submit a query, one thing I've observed from sitting in on query workshops is that writers tend to cram everything into a page. Try to keep in mind that a query letter is an advertisement. The query letter's job is to get an agent to ask to read the manuscript (just like an advertisement's job is to get you to click through to a landing page, or pick up the phone to call now). Your job isn't to summarize the book. Your job is to sell the book. Try writing the query letter like the marketing copy on the back of published books.

As you saw in part one of this book, querying can be a numbers game. Agents are completely inundated by all the would-be writers—everyone in the middle and outside rings from my introduction. They're getting thousands of queries a year and only take on a few new authors. I don't have an answer for bypassing the numbers game, and would suggest that plenty of very good books don't find an agent due to sheer bad luck. Maybe you queried the perfect agent on the day before they leave for vacation, and your query got lost. Or maybe you query on the day after they've accepted not one but three projects, and, out of time, they sent blanket rejections to every outstanding query in their inbox. In part one I suggested one in 10,000 was a useful a statistic for weighing the odds of getting a traditional book deal, but that doesn't mean you need to send 10,000 query letters. I'm confident in saying that if you have a truly good book, you'll be in the top 10%—still not a comforting statistic but one to keep your hope alive.

One way to meet agents is to attend a writers conference. That can get expensive, but is worth doing once if you can swing it. Conferences may set up an in-person pitch session for you with an agent, usually five to ten minutes. I've stood in line for these things, and I've seen writers shaking out of concern. Relax. An agent is extremely unlikely to pluck you out of the slush pile at the conference and send you on a path to fame and fortune. At best, they'll tell you the book sounds interesting and send it their way. Instead of thinking of these pitch sessions as your One Big Shot, try to think of them as a chance for you to interview an agent, get a little feedback on your pitch, and gain some information about how they operate. It's market research that you can then take back and use when you start querying agents en masse.

And if you don't get a great response from your queries? If you send a bunch of queries but don't get anyone asking to read the manuscript, your query needs work. If people are reading your manuscript but rejecting you, your book project may not scream bestseller, or it may have major editorial issues. Try to figure out if you need to revise, or if you need to go a different route—either querying small presses directly, or writing another, more commercial book. You may also want to consider hiring a freelance editor. A good book editor isn't cheap ($1,000 or more) but can clear up a number of issues you inevitably see in early-career novels.

181

I recently saw a blog post from a literary agent about what to do when you get an offer of representation. The post had a laundry list of tasks—from reaching out to other agents who might have your book under consideration to conducting interviews and ultimately "finalizing the deal." This agent, who seems fine and well meaning, made Getting. An. Agent. sound like winning *The Bachelor*, a "monumental step in your career." Given the experiences I've laid out in this book, and given what I know about other authors in that middle ring from my preface, the book industry at large and agents in particular do authors a disservice by placing so much emphasis on Getting. An. Agent.

Yes, it can be an important step in your career—if you get lucky. But I would add the counter-argument that agents are not your savior, and you probably shouldn't spend too much energy worrying about them. If you have a great book with high sales potential, finding an agent shouldn't be too difficult. If you're having trouble finding an agent, it's probably because your book is in the wide middle of "perfectly good books that don't scream bestseller." You might get lucky and find an agent, or you might waste a ton of time when you'd be better served either finding a different route to publication or writing another book.

To make matters worse, plenty of people (myself included) sign with an agent but their book doesn't sell. There's limited data about how often this happens, but one agent has told me it happens "all the time." Publishing is a tough business for everyone. Things that might go wrong with your agent relationship include:

- You've got a great book and a great agent, but it doesn't sell. This can be bad luck, or the genre you're working in is worn out for now, or political winds shift, or the perfect editor for you came down with the flu and mass-rejected 100 items in their inbox. Your great agent is encouraging but realistic and has an open conversation with you about what next.

- Your agent is, shall we say, less strategic or well connected. After shot-gunning it out to 20 editors, they tell you it's not going to sell, sorry pal. Maybe they get out of the business altogether, leaving you back at square one but out a couple of years in your too-short life.

- Your book sells 2,000 copies in hardback which puts you into the anonymous midlist, and your publisher passes on your next book. If your agent has courage, they let you know they're also dropping you for your next book. If they don't have courage, they hem and haw and say "good work," but reply more and more slowly to your emails and seem to generally forget about you until you eventually fire them.

- Your book sells for a decent amount of money and does decently well in the market, but you didn't secure a multi-book deal, which means you're homeless on the market. Your next book is not a repeat of the first book, so your agent tells you to write something else (and maybe gives you an outline of what they want you to write), or they decide to drop you (or passive-aggressively wait for you to fire them).

- Your book sells way too well, and after your second book fails to earn out your advance, your two-book contract is over and you're homeless on the market. Your third book is too weird or whatever, so your agent tells you to write something else (or drops you).

Some of these scenarios have happened to me; others have happened to friends of mine. These are the scenarios industry people don't tell you about, but make sense when you consider the literary agent business model. They work on commission, so if you're not getting paid, they're not getting paid.

Remember the concentric rings I opened this book with? Agents want to represent writers in the center ring because that is where the money is. If you can't get an agent, it's likely because no one you query can envision your book getting you into that center ring. This business structure creates a few wonky incentives for agents that are not necessarily in a novelist's best interest. For instance, if you give your agent a literary book that might be perfect for a medium-sized independent press, with maybe a $1,000 advance, your agent might send you back to the drawing board. Does that mean the book is no good? Nope. It means it's not worth their time to do anything with it. If you receive a

$1,000 advance, your agent receives $150 on commission. If they spend more than about two hours on the book, they're losing money—in fact, they're losing money just by taking time to read your book. Remember, agents are in business just like everyone else. At a 15% commission, they need to focus on book deals with five- and six-figure advances to be able to pay rent, particularly if they live in New York.

Key point: If you're getting rejected by agents, all that means is that your book isn't a likely candidate for a five-figure advance.

Finally, I should acknowledge before moving on that my career, as you read in part one, didn't work out with the literary agent path. I opened this book with a quote from Kierkegaard, "Subjectivity is truth," and my truth is obviously skewing my perspective. I've been frustrated over the years, but think I'm being honest when I say I don't have an ax to grind here. Agents are in business, and publishing is an almost impossible business to be in. The only way forward is either to quit or keep going. Keep querying, but also consider writing another book.

PUBLISHERS

Who are these mysterious publishers whose editors "do lunch" with agents, and who pay five- and six-figure advances for your little old book? Can you submit your book to a publisher directly? Today, you generally have three options for publication: (1) traditional publishers, (2) hybrid publishers, and (3) self-publishing.

I. Traditional publishers buy the rights to your work and offer a royalty as payment. Quite often, traditional publishers will pay you an advance against royalties, which means you get an up-front fee that is then deducted from your royalties as the book sells. Your job after that is to work with the publisher on editing, and to help promote the book, but the publisher pays for all of the book production costs. It's the same idea as if you invented a widget, got a patent on it, and then a company bought the intellectual property rights for said patent. The company would pay to commercialize and sell it and provide you whatever payment or royalty you arranged.

Traditional publishing can be grouped into three camps:

First, the "big five" New York publishers: Penguin Random House, HarperCollins, Hachette, MacMillan, and Little Brown. Each of these five publishers are actually conglomerates that have a variety of "imprints." For instance, MacMillan imprints include Farrar Strauss Giroux (a highly literary imprint), Henry Holt (a somewhat general imprint), Picador (paperback books), St. Martin's Press (an imprint of more popular books), Minotaur (crime fiction), et cetera. The idea is that each imprint is a kind of brand or product line, the same way Proctor & Gamble has a variety of divisions and then brands within those divisions.

To sell a book to one of the big five, you will need an agent. For most novelists, a big traditional publisher still offers the biggest advantage, in that they have the most money and the largest network of distribution. If you're writing straightforward genre (e.g., romance, fantasy) and can write quickly, you might do better self-publishing, but to get into bookstores and have movies made of your books, you'll probably find yourself with a traditional publisher.

Second, big independent publishers: Houghton Mifflin, Norton, Grove, and a few other publishers are not part of the big five, but they largely operate the same way. They may have multiple imprints, and you will need an agent to sell to them. Independent publishing operates on something of a spectrum. I might put Graywolf, Coffee House Books, Europa, Soho, Melville House, and a few others in this mid-sized camp. These companies are all independent publishers, but they are well enough established and have a large enough reach in the book trade that you might be familiar with them, you can likely find at least a few of their titles in most bookstores, and you probably need an agent to sell a book to them.

Finally, small publishing, university publishing, and micro-publishing: there are countless publishers out there, some very good and some downright terrible. It might not be fair to lump them all together, but what I would say is that this third camp is generally where you will go if you don't have an agent representing you. Some of these presses offer strong distribution, their books get good publicity, you can often find their titles in stores, and more and more they are relying on agented submissions. Other publishers in this camp are print-on-demand (POD) operations whose titles may only be found through the press website and on Amazon.

I can't tell you how to evaluate the publishers in this third camp, because your evaluation is going to depend largely on your own goals. A university press can be a highly respected outlet and may be the best option if you are in academia writing for primarily academic audiences. University presses will get your books into university libraries and to a small segment of the general book trade, but they seldom break out with the public at large. A micro press (500 or fewer sales) may be a great option if you write something highly specific (e.g., fairy tale flash fiction) or if you are writing something highly localized that may be of interest to a few counties but not the rest of the country.

If you're hoping to break out with the general public beyond your home town, I would look at how long the press has been in business, what kind of distribution they have (more on that below), and whether your book would fit well on the shelf with other titles. The neat thing about small presses is that if they are doing a good job, they fill a specific niche. Haywire Books, for instance, is a traditional small press. I'm still trying to work out the exact niche, but I would say that if you like one book in the catalog, you'll likely enjoy others. There is a unique flavor for every small press, so your job is to find a press that fits your book.

II. Hybrid publishing is a somewhat new category, and the term still seems fluid. What I understand it to be is a model by which the press buys the rights to publish and sell your book, but you as the author have to pay into the system. You might invest several thousand dollars, but the publishing contract gives you a higher royalty rate than a traditional publisher (whereas a traditional publisher may offer a royalty of 8% the suggested retail price, a hybrid publisher may offer up to 50%). She Writes Press, BQB Publishing, and Life in 10 Minutes are three examples of presses in this mold.

Because the model is still somewhat new, it's tough to evaluate. Hybrid publishers do seem to have a screening process, which sets them apart from self-publishing, and it allows them to build a brand within the book trade. It costs a lot of money to put out a book properly, so asking the author to have a financial stake in it gives these presses a path to commercial viability. But, because there is so little profit in publishing, I'm not sure how authors ever get a return on the investment even with a much higher royalty rate. That said, you also won't see a return on investment from driving all over tarnation to promote your book from a traditional publisher, either. If you think about this as an investment today to build your career for the long haul, a hybrid publisher could be worth considering.

III. Self-publishing means you retain all the rights to your book, and you do the necessary work to get it into the hands of readers. This can be as simple as converting your Word document into a PDF and putting it up for sale on your own website, or as complicated as printing and warehousing books and finding a way to get them into the traditional book trade. At rock bottom, there are essentially two critical people in the book business: the author and the reader. Self-publishing theoretically offers you the ability to eliminate some of the middlemen to get directly to your readers, but in practice this is much, much harder than it sounds.

The rules of self-publishing are still being written, but I would offer a few ways of thinking about it. The most important issue is "discoverability." In 2018, around 1.68 million books were self-published, which translates into more than 4,500 books per day. How are you going to get any attention for your book? I see five possibilities:

1. You have a wide network of eager potential buyers. Richmond author Karen Chase self-published her novel *Carrying Independence* to good success because she was actively involved in the Daughters of the American Revolution, the target audience for her novel.

2. Your book is something people will search for. If I wrote a book called *How to Start a Freelance Copywriting Business*, and I optimized my website and retail sales pages with keywords, people would find the book when they search for the topic.

3. You become an expert in advertising. Amazon, Facebook, and Bookbub ads can get a book in front of a targeted group of readers. Getting the demographics right and making sure your ads are profitable is an entire business lesson in itself.

4. You belong to a strong online community. The fantasy, science fiction, and romance genre communities seem particularly strong, wide, and supportive. The self-publishing success stories you hear about (e.g., Hugh Howie, Amanda Hocking) came out of these communities.

5. You write a series. Another Richmond author, David Kazzie, found success in self-publishing his dystopic thriller *The Immune* as a series of four novels plus a collected omnibus edition. When you write a series, you can set the e-book price for part one at zero or $0.99 to get lots of readers, and a predictable number of those readers will move on to part two, and then part three, and so forth. This seems to be the biggest money-making trick for doing well as a self-published author. Write a series.

If you have a plan, it can be advantageous to self-publish because you maintain control of your rights and the means of production, but I wouldn't recommend this route unless you fully understand the system you are participating in and also have an entrepreneurial mindset. Kindlepreneur is a good online resource to start understanding this world, so I would recommend reading through that site's archives for your initial research. You may also want to check out the English spy writer Mark Dawson, who has an entire side business around advertising self-published books.

EDITORIAL & PRODUCTION

If you go the traditional route in publishing, your first stop will be an acquisitions editor, the person who will buy your book for the publishing house. This person may have the sole authority to make an offer, or they may have to take your book to some kind of board for a discussion. I once heard an editor say that the book business involves getting a bunch of people excited about a book—the agent, the editor, the board or publisher, the marketing people, book reviewers, booksellers, influencers, and finally the reading public.

Your acquisitions editor may also be the developmental editor. This level of editing is a macro look at the manuscript, and may involve wholesale revisions. Much developmental editing happens with agents today, rather than in the publishing house, as publishers are seeking out more "finished" books. By the time an agent submits a book, it's pretty well baked at the macro level.

For myself, the developmental editing for *The Whiskey Baron* was about structure. I had a number of plotlines and recurring character points of view, and my editor noted that the balance felt off. I would go a hundred pages where one major character would disappear. My macro-level revisions were about fixing the balance. For *The Edge of America*, my primary developmental editing happened with my agent. I went back and forth with my agent for several drafts. His big-picture concern was that the story was so complicated, it read like a Rube Goldberg machine and needed a guide, a character who could be making sense of the story along with the reader. I invented a private investigator who ended up becoming one of the central characters in the book. My investigator wasn't in the first five or so drafts of the book at all.

After developmental editing, you'll go through line editing, which may also be the step of copyediting (or, line editing may be administered with the developmental edit). Line editing and copyediting are at the sentence level, and include everything from adding nuance within a scene, to tightening up the perspective or psychic distance, to making sure you don't overuse words or phrases, to creating a unified style within the book (i.e., Chicago Style, AP Style). Fact-checking may occur in here too.

Finally, your book will go to proofreading. Once the book is laid out, you'll receive galleys (which may be the advanced review copies, or ARCs). This may be the final chance to review the book and check for any editorial issues before the first print run.

Then, you're done and the book is out of your hands.

While your book is going through editing, the marketing and publicity team will get to work. Every publisher is different, but they may kick things off with a meeting about the book's positioning. They may have you fill out a marketing survey to get a sense of your network and contacts—also known as your platform. From there, they will write your marketing copy for the back cover; start gathering endorsements, or blurbs, from other authors; and design the book cover. Depending on the size of the publishing house, you may have some input here, but most publishers consider book design to be their purview. They're the ones marketing a product, whereas you may want to create a work of art. In these meetings, the editor or publicity team may suggest you change your title. Or, they may assign you a new title that they believe will be more marketable.

When your book is complete and laid out, the publicity team will print your ARCs and start distributing them to reviewers, booksellers, and other "influencers." A sample of these include the trade review publications (e.g., *Publishers Weekly, Kirkus Reviews, Library Journal*), industry trade shows (e.g., the Book Expo of America), and independent booksellers. They might give away copies on Goodreads or another forum to drum up reviews, and then they'll start sending it out to consumer reviewers, such as at newspapers or magazines.

The entire process from acceptance to publication might take a year to eighteen months, with six months to a year being reserved for the various stages of editing and six months for marketing.

PUBLICITY

The realm of publicity is where careers are made and hearts are broken. Industry people talk about discoverability as being the greatest challenge to marketing a book. As many as 4,500 books are published every day, and consumers have limitless ways to spend their time, so how will you get your book noticed? Your publisher—large or small—likely has several publicity levers they can pull, from sending promotional copies to potential reviewers to calling up booksellers to organize a book tour. But much of the onus these days falls on authors, and for mainstream publicity, money talks.

Once the book is published, you'll probably have a launch party and send out a ton of obnoxious tweets and emails. You might go on book tour, and you'll probably set up a Google Alerts for yourself and read every review. Then, you have the big moment for potential heartbreak. After publication, you've got about three months for the book to take off on its own legs. I'd compare the initial marketing blitz to a bomb going off. Your publicity team is trying to get your book noticed in a crowded field, and get it into the hands of readers. If it all goes according to plan—positive trade reviews, bookseller interest, maybe a few "best of the season" lists—enough readers will pick up the book that a self-sustaining chain reaction occurs.

To supplement their publisher's efforts, many authors hire freelance publicists (out of their own savings or their advance money from the publisher), and there does seem to be some correlation between your publicity budget and a book's success. How much does a publicist cost? A basic package may start around $5,000, which will get you a book tour, some media and bookseller outreach, and maybe a few good ideas. I've heard it's not uncommon for bigger name literary writers—the writers in the inner ring I laid out in my preface—to invest $10,000 to $15,000 of their own money in publicity, which might get you a review in the *New York Times*, whereas a $30,000 investment might get you onto the finalist list for a major book prize. My understanding of publicity budgets is all hearsay, but I feel confident in saying that the traditional literary world is not a meritocracy. Aptitude and hard work only get you so far, and beyond that you need luck. In the realm of publicity, money buys a lot of luck—at least when a book first comes out.

For long-term success, most book sales happen via referral. An investment of $30,000 may get you a few national reviews and a shortlist for the National Book Awards, but after the initial months of attention, a book's success lies with readers themselves. Maybe an indie bookseller recommends a book, or maybe you see a review in *O Magazine*, but most likely what happens is someone recommends a book to you. Or your book club picks it. Or you see it face-out on the shelf at the library. The marketing push only does so much, and the bad news is that if big success hasn't happened in three months, it likely won't happen—at least not in any dramatic, noticeable way. After three months, the booksellers will pull the title off the new releases shelf, and they may start returning copies to the distributor (books are sold returnable in this business, which is an old and unfortunate system—at least for authors and publishers). If your book isn't short-listed for any awards and you don't appear on any end-of-year lists, your best bet may be to focus on the next book. You can keep booking events— going from indie booksellers to festivals to, maybe, colleges or libraries. And you can keep posting obnoxious links about it on social media, but the best way for you to sell more copies of the book at this point is to write another book. *The Whiskey Baron* hadn't sold much at all for years, but when *The Edge of America* came out, I sold almost as many copies of my first book as I did for the new one.

THE BOOK TRADE

There is one more suite of middlemen between you and your reader, and this middleman is "the book trade." When a publisher finishes production on a book, they send it to a printer for a print run. Some smaller presses may upload files for POD, but I suspect even those publishers will print a hundred copies or so to get the initial sales going.

Print-on-demand operations don't require warehousing, and the rules around distribution and fulfillment are different, but for publishers selling more than, say, 500 copies, they'll probably do a print run. Once you have 500 or 5,000 copies of the book printed, the publisher has to put them somewhere. Big publishers like Penguin Random House might do their own distribution, which means they'll warehouse the book themselves. Smaller publishers might use a distributor like Consortium or Publishers Group West. These publishers will send the print run to the distribution warehouse.

As the book is marketed, wholesalers and retailers will start placing orders, and the distributor will fulfill those orders. Amazon's great disruption is to be a wholesaler and retailer, so the distributor will send copies directly to Amazon. The other wholesalers are Baker & Taylor (primarily library sales) and Ingram (primarily bookstores). Ingram may order a certain number of copies, and the distributor will send those boxes to various regional warehouses. Indie booksellers and other retailers will place their orders from Ingram, and Ingram will ship copies to bookstores around the country where you, the intrepid reader, walk in and purchase a copy.

I bring up the book trade for two reasons. First, if you are evaluating small presses, distribution is a key thing to look at. Most reputable publishers of fiction find a way to distribute into the full book trade, meaning they can get their books into Ingram's system. If the press doesn't sell into Ingram (or doesn't use Ingram's POD system), independent bookstores will not carry your book. Your local store may agree to carry a few copies on consignment, but if you want to be on bookstore shelves at large, your publisher needs distribution.

A second reason understanding the book trade and the distribution system matters is because of money. You can see from the above description just how many players are in the book industry, and how many times a print book goes from one location to another: the printer to a distributor, and then from a distributor to a wholesalers, and then from a wholesaler to a retailer. The freight costs alone eat up a significant portion of a book's cover price.

The self-publishing community has made strides over the past ten years in bypassing some of these middlemen, and there is an entire ecosystem of self-published authors who upload their books to Amazon and nowhere else, and then use a combination of Amazon, Facebook, and Bookbub advertising to find their audience. That is one viable pathway for a novelist, and it can be lucrative if you have the entrepreneurial mindset and also get lucky. But the system of the book trade generally operates more like an interconnected car engine than a linear A to B process. By this I mean, you can't really take out one component (e.g., the distributor) without losing out on some of the benefits of the rest of the trade (e.g., the retailer).

If your publisher is participating in the entire book trade, the money is cut among numerous players on standard terms. For example, the chart below demonstrates where the money would go for a $20 book sold in your local bookstore:

$8	40% retail discount (the bookstore cut)
$3	15% wholesaler fee
$1-2	Freight
$1-2	Distribution and warehousing fee
$2-3	Printing
$1-3	Publisher revenue
$1.50	Author royalty ($0.22 fee for your agent)

This breakdown is for print books that are traditionally published and distributed through the book trade. E-books and audio books have their own set of numbers, but you can see there isn't a whole lot of room for give in the system. It's not as though publishers are rolling in profits (though the bigger publishers benefit greatly from economy of scale). It's not as though UPS or FedEx is suddenly going to start delivering boxes of books for less money, when they have all the other consumer products to deliver. Retailers get a big piece of the pie, but when you start doing the math about what it takes to operate a bookstore—all the overhead and labor costs—and you look at profits of $8 per book, you realize they have to sell tens of thousands of books a year to keep the lights on.

What all this means is that your book, for it to be a profit-able endeavor for a publisher and your agent and yourself, needs to sell many, many copies. More copies than you have people in your personal network. You need a ton of strangers to fork over their money and their time, and therein lies the great difficulty of being a professional novelist.

DISRUPTION

I've said again and again in this book that publishing is a tough business, and would-be novelists have a long road in front of them. One big challenge—and, possibly, opportunity—is broader cultural shifts that have occurred in the 21st century. If I had to lay out succinctly what makes being a novelist today so difficult, I would point to two things:

1. Supply: We have too many people trying to be novelists.
2. Demand: Would-be readers have too many other things to do besides read novels.

On the supply side, how many would-be novelists such as myself had the privilege to go to college in the 1990s or 2000s and take a creative writing class, and then decided that would be a good career path? The avenues of self-publishing have democratized entry to the field, but it's also created competition in the form of noise. Every story may matter, but in a world of endless supply, not every story can have economic value. They don't call economics the "dismal science" for nothing.

On the demand side, it's a great time to be a consumer in the 21st century, if nothing else for the volume of affordable entertainments at your disposal. If you were to make a pie chart for how people spend their days, you'd have a big chunk for sleep, a big chunk for work, a chunk for socializing, and a chunk for entertainment and media. Fifty years ago, the media chunk was limited to three TV networks, books, newspapers, magazines, and radio. Today, that chunk is fractured in to a thousand pieces, ranging from Five-Thirty-Eight election coverage to Buzzfeed listicles to streaming TV and new social media platforms like TikTok.

Books are a smaller piece of the pie.

To make matters worse, the nature of work in the 21st century has changed. In corporate America, executives and HR people talk a big game about "work-life balance," but I would argue "work-life integration" is a better term for what's happening. Thanks to smart phones and Wi-Fi, we are able to work flexibly and remotely, but we are also connected all hours of the day. Few jobs are clock-in, clock-out operations, which means people in corporate America put their kids to bed and then spend the evening catching up on emails or projects they couldn't get to during a day full of meetings at the office. The hours that used to be about leisure are about work—catching up when you're swamped, or business development, or networking, or building your personal brand. Instead of reading a novel over lunch, today's worker bees are scarfing down sandwiches in their cars between meetings, ticking through emails (or, reading about the latest political drama).

The "entertainment" slice of the pie is smaller and more fractured. Consumers are harder to reach and harder to hold, yet there are more novelists trying to get attention than ever before. That, in a nutshell, is why publishing is such a tough industry.

Because of these challenges, the industry is undergoing "disruption," one of the business world's words-of-the-moment going into the 2020s. Some of the disruption is around channels and access. Amazon's print-on-demand KDP platform and Ingram's Spark platform allow novelists (or "content creators") to upload books in a matter of minutes. Over a long weekend, you can take a Word document, design a cover for it using an online template, upload it to a program that will format it as an e-book, set a price, and have a book for sale anywhere in the book trade. You will still face the challenge of building a readership, but anyone with an internet connection and some know-how can publish a book.

I'm of two minds about this. I believe democratization can generally be a force for good, as gatekeepers in power often reinforce old (and sometimes unjust) power structures. But, the same kind of democratization has happened all over the media landscape. With blogs and social media, anyone can be a "citizen journalist." The promise of citizen journalism could be seen at the beginning of the Arab Spring, where everyday people connected, organized, and shared information. The downside of citizen journalism—and of getting rid of gatekeepers—can be seen in the decline of old-fashioned credible journalism, and the way so many news bombshells end up getting walked back or clarified a few days later. You take away the gatekeepers, and you open up a world of fake news in which the populace is manipulated by nefarious forces rigging the system. Who's to say anything I've said in this book is the "truth"? You have my say-so, and there is a legal framework in the United States in which libel, slander, and plagiarism are crimes. It's not a crime, however, for me to tell you that 2 + 2 = 5. Because I can self-publish, my good name and my inherent commitment to the truth are really the only things standing between me and a cynical manipulation of readers.

Even more insidious, as we head into the 2020s, the mainstream media outlets themselves are trying to compete with all this noise. Speculation and innuendo are dwarfing actual objective news in just about every news outlet in business today. The media needs a story, but without any real news to report, the media will put out breathless headlines about what is possible, what the story *might* be. Then, these headlines take off, and the story gains traction, and pretty soon the possible becomes reality—yet the media machine absolves itself of any accountability. This phenomenon is not new—the boom and bust of the business cycle is often driven by mood and speculation—but what is new is the way the media cycle has become so front and center in the minds of everyday Americans. We are addicted to news, and if the mainstream media isn't giving us our fix, there are countless citizen-journalists running blogs or alt-media sites or Twitter feeds to fill the gap.

In such an environment, truth is the ultimate liability, because innuendo captures consumer eyeballs in a way that dry facts do not. Truth is one reason I believe fiction still matters. By definition, fiction is a lie, but within the lie of a fictional story you can find some greater truth, something bigger than the author and the reader. Stories are what help us make sense of a chaotic world, and unlike stories in the media, which are driving the construction of "truth," stories in fiction construct out of hindsight. We write novels slowly, carefully, to discover a story, and therefore discover—rather than manufacture—the truth. While fiction writers can manipulate readers to some degree—such as short paragraphs to speed up the pacing and maybe quicken the pulse to create suspense—you ultimately are advancing a point of view. A writer of intelligence, sensitivity, and humility can advance a greater truth within the lie of a fiction.

I'll end this book where I started it, with a return to Kierkegaard's contention that "Subjectivity is truth," along with its corollary that "Truth is subjectivity." My understanding of this view is that in the world according to Kierkegaard, you cannot separate objective truth from the subjective experience. Truth is an inward leap of faith, an orientation of the self toward some higher reality. As a novelist, your readers are swirling in a culture and their own histories, which they will bring to bear when they read your book. Your job is to give them a true story, one that will reorient them in a world gone haywire.

Good luck.

NOTES

PREFACE

1   Jon Sealy, "So You Want to Be a Novelist." Published in *The Millions* (Sept. 26, 2019).

2   Henry James, *The Aspern Papers*. In chapter VII, the character discusses his fortune (or lack thereof) with his landlord, who asks him if he sells the books he writes. He replies, "Do you mean don't people buy them? A little—not so much as I could wish. Writing books, unless one be a great genius—and even then!—is the last road to fortune. I think there is no more money to be made by literature."

3   "Subjectivity is truth." Søren Kierkegaard, *Concluding Unscientific Postscript to Philosophical Fragments*.

    Ernest Hemingway's quote originated in *The Paris Review* (Issue 18, Spring 1958).

THE CAREER

9   Flannery O'Connor, "The Nature and Aim of Fiction," collected in *Mystery and Manners: Occasional Prose* (FSG 1969).

14 Ron Rash, *One Foot in Eden* (Novello 2002, Picador paperback 2004).

    George Singleton, "This Itches, Y'all," collected in *The Half Mammals of Dixie* (Algonquin 2002).

15 Bret Lott explains his theory of fiction in his memoir, *Before We Get Started*, particularly the essay "Against Technique" (Ballantine 2005).

    O'Connor, "Writing Short Stories," *Mystery and Manners*.

16 James Baldwin, *No Name in the Street* (The Dial Press 1972, Vintage reissue 2007).

17 O'Connor, "The Nature and Aim of Fiction," *Mystery and Manners*.

21 Barry Hannah, "Passion to Brilliance," introduction to Larry Brown's *A Miracle of Catfish* (Algonquin 2007).

    Jonathan Miles, "Foreword" to Larry Brown's *Tiny Love: The Complete Stories* (Algonquin 2019).

22 George Singleton, *Pep Talks, Warnings, and Screeds* (Writers Digest Books 2008).

23 Stephen King, *On Writing: A Memoir of the Craft* (Simon & Schuster 2001).

27 Ted Solotaroff, "Writing in the Cold," *Granta* (March 1985).

29 William Gibson's quote has been circulating for decades in slightly different forms, but it seems to have originated in the late 1990s.

32 Samuel Beckett's quote comes from a short story called "Worstword Ho!" (1983). The context for the quote is perhaps less than inspiring. In the next paragraph, he writes, "Try again. Fail again. Better again. Or better worse. Fail worse again. Still worse again. Till sick for good. Throw up for good." The ending seems to be a wash: "At bounds of boundless void. Whence no farther. Best no worse no farther. Nohow less. Nohow worse. Nohow naught. Nohow on."

36 Steve Yarbrough, *The Unmade World* (Unbridled 2018).

Jami Attenberg, *All This Could Be Yours* (Houghton Mifflin 2019).

37 Emily St. John Mandel's first three novels—*Last Night in Montreal* (2009), *The Singer's Gun* (2010), and *The Lola Quartet* (2012)—were published by Unbridled. *Station Eleven* (2014) was published by Knopf, an enviable career arc. Another Unbridled alum, Peter Geye, moved to Knopf for his third book, *Wintering*.

39 Flaubert's quote about living like a bourgeois comes from a letter he wrote to Gertrude Tennant (December 25, 1876).

James Dickey's quip about advertising is from *The Paris Review* (Issue 65, Spring 1976).

William Carlos Williams's famous line "no ideas but in things" comes from his poem "Paterson," but has been used to describe his poetic philosophy.

40 Wallace Stevens's line "the palm at the end of the mind" comes from his poem "Of Mere Being," and was used as the title for his selected poems.

Agatha Christie references the Spanish proverb "Take what you want and pay for it, says God" in several Hercule Poirot novels. In what I assume is a nod to Christie, Tana French picks up the line in her novel *The Likeness*.

42 In season 2 of *The Wire*, the Greek drug dealer Spiros Vondas explains business as "buy for a nickel, sell for a dime."

43 Ann Patchett, "My Life in Sales," collected in *This Is the Story of a Happy Marriage* (HarperCollins 2013).

Emma Straub's interview—"Emma Straub's Life in Letters (So Far)" by Eryn Loeb—is in the September/October *Poets & Writers*.

46 Michael Chabon's commentary about the genre/literary divide may be found in his introduction to the *Best American Short Stories 2005* (Houghton Mifflin). He also discusses it in his introduction to *McSweeney's Mammoth Treasury of Thrilling Tales*, an anthology he edited in 2003.

47 A few examples of the public hand-wringing over the genre/literary divide include Steven Petite's "Literary Fiction vs. Genre Fiction" (*Huffington Post*, April 2014), Joshua Rothman's "A Better Way to Think About the Genre Debate" (*The New Yorker*, November 2014), and "How Genre Became More Important than Literary Fiction" (*Esquire*, March 2015). Seemingly

every bookish person in the country has felt the need to weigh in on that debate.

48 I believe the phrase "Rough South" stems from filmmaker Gary Hawkins, who produced the documentaries *The Rough South of Harry Crews* (1991) and *The Routh South of Larry Brown* (2002).

49 You can trace the decline of the idea of the "South" in the introductions to Algonquin's *New Stories from the South* anthology. In 2004, Tim Gautreaux wonders idly "why the American South is an important source of short fiction of distinctive literary quality." He then proceeds to make a number of generalizations ("Southern storytellers do love their cities" and "Southern writers love the short story form, too"). He's in tune enough to ask the question about the definition of the "South," but still seems to believe it exists as a unique thing.

In 2008, ZZ Packer made a distinction between a "Southerner" and a "southerner," arguing, "If being a southerner and not a Southerner means one is not quite so self-assured, it also guarantees some reflection, some twisted-arm compromise, a kind of double indemnity of the soul peculiar to thinking folk." In her introduction, there is a diminishment of the "South," something smaller yet more tactile and specific.

Then we get to 2010, the last year of the anthology, in which Amy Hempel writes, "So. Why was a Chicago-born writer who grew up in Colorado and California and has lived in New York City for the past many years asked to select the stories for this important anthology of short fiction from the South? *I was too thrilled at the invitation to ask!*" (italics are Hempel's). She has no answers for us, but adds, "Though one's sense of geography is keen, it's hard to feel there is much that separates us after reading the stories collected here." For Hempel, the "South" is a matter of geography rather than a generalized culture.

Perhaps the anthology ended in 2010 out of commercial reasons—the end of what some people termed a new golden age of the American short story—but it makes sense to me that it became too difficult to hold up a pillar of "Southern" literature when the cultural underpinning of the "South" had vanished.

50 Tom Franklin's second novel, *Smonk*, is essentially a Western set in rural Alabama, and was marketed as such. His first novel, *Hell at the Breech*, was marketed as a "southern" novel but also contains some of the hallmarks of a Western.

51 Daniel Woodrell's *Winter's Bone* was published in 2006. Ron Rash's "Back of Beyond" (*Tin House* 2007) was collected in *New Stories from the South* (2008) and his book *Burning Bright* (Ecco 2010). William Gay's "Where Will You Go When Your Skin Cannot Contain You" was published by *Tin House* in 2006 and anthologized in the *Best American Short Stories 2007*. I would argue these pieces were an authentic expression of what was

happening in America at the time (Art), but paved the way for imitators writing in a mode (Artifice).

"Tradition and the Individual Talent," *The Selected Prose of T.S. Eliot* (Harvest 1975), edited by Frank Kermode.

53   Arthur Conan Doyle killed Sherlock Holmes in the story "The Final Problem," but resurrected the detective in "The Adventure of the Empty House" following outrage from his readers.

Wilton Barnhardt, *Lookaway, Lookaway* (St. Martin's 2013).

54   Ray Kurzweill, *The Singularity Is Near* (Viking 2005).

55   Bill McKibben, *Falter: Has the Human Game Begun to Play Itself Out?* (Wildfire 2019).

56   Philip Roth's comment about consciousness is in Claudia Pierpont Roth's *Roth Unbound* (FSG 2013).

58   Lucy Ellmann's quote is from an interview with Sian Cain in *The Guardian* (Dec. 7, 2019).

65   The Henry James quote comes from his essay, "The Art of Fiction."

66   The best analysis of the Twitter mob that I have seen is Jon Ronson's *So You've Been Publicly Shamed* (Riverhead 2015).

67   The two most popular introductory powerlifting programs are Starting Strength (a book and program by Mark Rippetoe) and Strong Lifts 5x5 (a website and app run by a guy named Mehdi at stronglifts.com). Both programs are indebted to Bill Starr's 1970s football training manual, *The Strongest Shall Survive*.

69   Richard Rohr, *Falling Upward: A Spirituality for the Two Halves of Life* (Jossey Bass 2011).

74   The event with John Lane was in late 2015. His next book was a collection of poems, *Anthropocene Blues* (Mercer 2017).

77   George Singleton, *Staff Picks* (LSU 2019).

79   The quote from James Salter might be apocryphal, but the referenced critical biography is William Dowie's *James Salter* (Twayne 1998).

81   A page called "The Hogarth Press" on the British Library website argues, "The Woolfs decided that the Hogarth Press would concentrate on small and experimental publications likely to be of no interest to commercial publishers." The article also alleges Woolf was "hypersensitive to criticism," so the press "would give them to freedom to publish whatever they liked … [and] to continue developing her experimental style."

82   To read more about the mission and catalog, visit HaywireBooks.com.

THE CRAFT

86 O'Connor, "Writing Short Stories," *Mystery and Manners*.

87 Gertrude Stein's phrase comes from her book *Everybody's Autobiography*. Describing her childhood home in Oakland, California, she said, in a stream-of-consciousness, "What was the use of my having come from Oakland it was not natural to have come from there yes write about it if I like or anything if I like but not there, there is no there there."

O'Connor, "Total Effect and the Eighth Grade," *Mystery and Manners*.

96 Jane Smiley, *13 Ways of Looking at the Novel* (Knopf 2005).

98 E.L. Doctorow's quote about driving at night comes from *The Paris Review* (Issue 101, Winter 1986).

100 The Mark Rothko painting I have in mind is "Untitled," circa 1950.

101 Cormac McCarthy, *All the Pretty Horses* (Vintage paperback edition, 1993).

105 Timothy Spurgin, *The English Novel* (The Great Courses).

106 Jane Austen, *Pride & Prejudice*.

Russell Banks, *The Sweet Hereafter* (HarperCollins 1991).

107 F. Scott Fitzgerald, *The Great Gatsby*. The former fiction editor of Esquire, Rust Hills, discusses the role of Nick versus Gatsby in his book *Writing in General and the Short Story in Particular* (Houghton Mifflin 1977), in which he argues the "moved" character also aligns with the point-of-view character. For Hills, *The Great Gatsby* is about Nick.

109 In "The Art of Fiction," Henry James writes, "We must grant the artist his subject, his idea, what the French call his donné; our criticism is applied only to what he makes of it. Naturally I do not mean that we are bound to like it or find it interesting: in case we do not our course is perfectly simple—to let it alone." Great advice for every citizen-critic on Goodreads and Twitter.

111 John Gardner, *On Becoming a Novelist* (Norton Reprint Edition 1999).

113 Anton Chekhov's recommendation about the gun appears in a few different variations in his letters, and it has become a staple of writing advice.

113 David Foster Wallace, *Infinite Jest* (Back Bay Anniversary Edition 2006).

114 Kent Haruf, *Benediction* (Knopf 2013).

115 Elmore Leonard's *10 Rules of Writing* (an illustrated book published by William Morrow 2007) originally appeared as an essay in the *New York Times* (July 16, 2001). He wrote, "Try to leave out the part that readers tend to skip."

119 The video of Sharon McCrumb is titled "Pronouncing Appalachia" and is currently on YouTube (as of Feb. 2020).

120 James Wood, "Half Against Flaubert," *The Broken Estate* (Modern Library Edition 2000).

122 Ann Patchett, *Commonwealth* (HarperCollins 2016).

129 Gabriel Garcia Marquez, *One Hundred Years of Solitude* (Harper Perennial Reprint 2006). The novel is written in an omniscient voice, but there is at least one scene of close-up stream-of-consciousness, when one of the wives goes on a delightful multi-page rant.

130 Zadie Smith, *NW* (Penguin Paperback 2013).

131 Toni Morrison, *Jazz* (Vintage Reprint 2004).

Tana French, *Faithful Place* (Penguin Paperback 2011).

133 Min Jin Lee, *Pachinko* (Grand Central 2017).

134 Jami Attenberg, *The Middlesteins* (Houghton Mifflin 2012).

136 Tana French, *In the Woods* (Penguin Paperback 2008).

137 Gillian Flynn, *Gone Girl* (Broadway Paperback 2014).

138 The Hollywood mogul quote about irony appears to be apocryphal. I encountered it in Bret Lott's *Before We Get Started*.

Mark Twain, *The Adventures of Huckleberry Finn* (University of California Press Edition 2001).

142 John Keats praised Shakespeare's "negative capability" in a letter to George and Tom Keats (December 1817).

143 Henry James, *The Portrait of a Lady*. This novel is the quintessential "Jamesian" novel in which the drama hinges on a character's emerging consciousness. John Banville's *Mrs. Osmond* (Knopf 2017). offers an interesting take on what happens to Isabel after James ends the story.

144 Elena Ferrante's Neapolitan novels, published by Europa, are: *My Brilliant Friend, The Story of a New Name, Those Who Leave and Those Who Stay*, and *The Story of the Lost Child*. The four novels comprise one overarching story.

148 E.M. Forster, *Aspects of the Novel*.

150 Mohsin Hamid, *Exit West* (Riverhead Paperback 2018).

152 Jonathan Franzen, *Freedom* (FSG 2010). With the publication of this novel, Franzen became something of a lightning rod on Twitter. It seems to have begun with the novelist Jennifer Weiner calling out the *New York Times* for its effusive coverage of *Freedom* (and, as a corollary, the paper's neglect of other novelists, particularly women). This spawned a phenomenon journalists have called "Franzenfreude," which has become so vociferous that he can't even write an essay effusively praising Edith Wharton

in *The New Yorker* ("A Rooting Interest," Feb. 13, 2012) without people on Twitter calling him a misogynist. It's hard to tell whether people are willfully misreading him, jumping on the complaint bandwagon without reading him, or genuinely missed his point in that essay.

It's a fair point about gender equality in book coverage, but *Freedom* is nonetheless an extraordinary novel—and possibly one of the last of its kind. As the daily conversations around books and politics on Twitter demonstrate, readers no longer seem to have the patience or the intellectual wherewithal to engage with nuance, and without a market for such a book, would-be novelists will no longer have an incentive to put in the work necessary to write such a book. Why would you? Why even bother trying to do something of consequence? The best advice these days might be to start a TikTok account and make cat videos.

156 In season 3 of *Bosch*, undercover FBI agent Luke Goshen tells the L.A. detective Bosch, "I envy the clarity of your mission, Bosch. Somebody's dead, and somebody did it." That line sums up the mystery genre in a nutshell.

157 Louise Penny, *Still Life* (St. Martin's/Minotaur Paperback 2008). I don't know if I'm the only one, but I have a hard time picturing anyone but David Suchet, who played Hercule Poirot on *Masterpiece Mystery*, as Penny's Chief Inspector Gamache. You could do worse than steal a classic character type.

160 Philip Roth, *The Ghost Writer* (Vintage Reprint Edition 1995). Again, the best read on Roth that I have encountered comes from Claudia Pierpont Roth's *Roth Unbound*, a kind of biography of his works. In addition to her own interviews, she cites two major sources for Roth-isms: his *Paris Review* interview (Issue 93, Fall 1984), and a series of online video interviews he did with Web of Stories (webofstories.com)—both great resources.

166 Richard Hugo, *The Triggering Town* (Norton 1979).

168 Edward P. Jones said in numerous interviews (*The Rumpus*, Politics & Prose, *AWP Writer*, among others) that he carried *The Known World* around in his head for ten years, only writing a few scenes. He told the *AWP Writer* interviewer he sat down to do the actual writing in 2001, and the novel was published in late 2003.

I first met Virginia Pye at the James River Writers "Writing Show" in Richmond, Virginia, in 2013. In an interview (or possibly a panel discussion), she described her process for writing *River of Dust*.

170 Don DeLillo's quote comes from—where else?—an interview with *The Paris Review* (Issue 128, Fall 1993).

171 Jeanine Cummins, *American Dirt* (Flatiron 2020). It's difficult to know where to start in picking apart this scandal. On the one hand, Flatiron has marketed the book as "the great American novel," complete with a

seven-figure advance, multiple reviews and profiles in the *New York Times*, and blurbs from top-tier authors Stephen King and Don Winslow. On its release day, Oprah selected it for her book club, but soon back-peddled to acknowledge the controversy.

Meanwhile, a suite of authors (most prominently Myriam Gurba and David Bowles) have critiqued the novel's presentation of Mexican culture and argued Cummins did not do justice to the story. Some of the critique has been rooted in the #OwnVoices movement—arguing that Cummins, who is white, is using Mexican trauma for her own gain at the expense of authors who are telling the same story authentically. Much of the critique is that Cummins, it seems, simply did a poor job in capturing the story, instead relying on stereotypes and clichés. In other words, it's a badly written book masquerading as high art.

Finally, Flatiron had a tasteless marketing campaign around the novel. The publisher held a swanky dinner to woo booksellers, and created a table centerpiece of the book cover and barbed wire. (Imagine, while promoting a book about the Holocaust, you had a showerhead as your centerpiece.) Additionally, the editor's letter indicated Cummins was married to an undocumented immigrant, without mentioning that he was an immigrant from Ireland. One of the biggest tragedies in all of this is that, rather than forcing the industry to take a hard look at itself, the scandal rocketed *American Dirt* to the top of the bestseller charts.

172 Alexander Chee, "How to Unlearn Everything," *Vulture* (Oct. 30, 2019).

173 Jonathan Franzen, "10 Rules for Novelists," *Lit Hub* (Nov. 15, 2018).

THE BUSINESS

187 The statistic about 4,500 books being published per day comes from the *Publishers Weekly* article "Number of Self-Published Titles Jumped 40% in 2018" (Oct. 15, 2019). Bowker (the company that administers ISBNs) issued a report that said 1.68 million self-published print and e-books were published in 2018, which translates into 4,600 books per day. This figure does not include traditionally published books. If you search for "books published per year," several websites cite a UNESCO statistic that about 300,000 books are traditionally published every year in the U.S.

194 There is much more to unpack about finances in the book business. Thomas Carlyle called economics "the dismal science," and unfortunately the hard truth is there is little money in publishing, which can create some odd social and political alliances. I'll end these notes with the oblique suggestion that if you want to understand the book business, a good place to start might be with the maxim, "Nobody knows anything."

Jon Sealy is the publisher of Haywire Books
and the author of *The Whiskey Baron, The
Edge of America,* and *The Merciful.* He lives in
Richmond, Virginia.

CPSIA information can be obtained
at www.ICGtesting.com
Printed in the USA
FSHW010712260321
79848FS